The Sacred Body Factories

Betsy Adams (Shoh Nah Hah Lieh)

BALBOA.
PRESS

A DIVISION OF HAY HOUSE

ISBN: 978-1-4525-5474-7 (sc)
ISBN: 978-1-4525-5473-0 (e)

Library of Congress Control Number: 2012911854

Balboa Press books may be ordered through booksellers or by contacting:

Balboa Press
A Division of Hay House
1663 Liberty Drive
Bloomington, IN 47403
www.balboapress.com
1-(877) 407-4847

Because of the dynamic nature of the Internet, any web addresses or links contained in this book may have changed since publication and may no longer be valid. The views expressed in this work are solely those of the author and do not necessarily reflect the views of the publisher, and the publisher hereby disclaims any responsibility for them.

The author of this book does not dispense medical advice or prescribe the use of any technique as a form of treatment for physical, emotional, or medical problems without the advice of a physician, either directly or indirectly. The intent of the author is only to offer information of a general nature to help you in your quest for emotional and spiritual well-being. In the event you use any of the information in this book for yourself, which is your constitutional right, the author and the publisher assume no responsibility for your actions.

Any people depicted in stock imagery provided by Thinkstock are models, and such images are being used for illustrative purposes only.

Certain stock imagery © Thinkstock.

Printed in the United States of America

Balboa Press rev. date: 7/19/2012

Previous works by Betsy Adams (Shoh Nah Hah Lleh)

Experimental Poetry and Prose

Histories

Losing the Moon 4,3,2,1 . .

Face at the bottom of the world

the dead birth, itself

Non Fiction

selfLove and the Healing of Our Animal Friends

Acknowledgements to those who made possible the creation of this work:

Each and every being I have met upon my way in this lifetime and in the many lifetimes my Soul

has chosen to explore here, has contributed to this work; for each and every being has been a

mirror for all my experiences here in this Ego Field we are all co-creating together. I want to

thank you all, and tell you how much I Love and Appreciate you and how fortunate I Feel in my

Heart and Soul that we have had this opportunity to explore Life in such a profound manner.

This work is dedicated to H., with much Love and Gratitude

As my friend and mentor, Michael Innocence said to me, loudly, many many many years ago:

"Remember the Body Factories!..."

Table of Contents   The Sacred Body Factories

Introduction to The Sacred Body Factories

We are, each of us, animal and human and plant and many other forms, creations of The Sacred Body Factories; these Gifts of God, of the Cosmos founded in the Love and the Metaphysics of Creation of Form. Love Is Formless and carries within All Creative Potential. And Love Loves, and in this Loving, this Giving Forth Creates the manifold and myriad Creations of Form. The Sacred Body Factories are trillions of years, eons and eons old, ancient and like everything that manifests has an "evolution" . . . i.e., depending upon events, free will choices, CHANGE occurs. And depending on the environment within which the form changes, very unique evolutions are occurring all over our Universe, all over the billions and trillions of Universes... let's say Infinite Universes! For the only "limit" to Creation of a Universe is the Will of the Divine, and the Divine is Infinite and it thus follows there are Infinite Universes.

There have been, in our own Universe, and especially on Planet Earth (which we are all really interested in!) unique evolutionary unfoldings. In order to enhance and aid these unique evolutionary presentations, the relationship between the Sacred Body Factories and what is needed for evolution here on Earth can be monitored, can be experienced, can be felt and learned about... if only we will ask for such insight. And trust we will receive!

For myself, I am given dreams, visions, actual 3D experiences of how the Sacred Body Factories create what manifests here as "forms" that we inhabit, that we share, that we can relate through and about our unique world : Earth, Nature, all Her inhabitants, and ultimately our

Universe which shares with us the Gifts of the Sacred Body Factories.

There are many levels of manifestation that occur, the Sacred Body Factories in conjunction

with the Soul of each being Co-Create these levels and these manifestations. We are NOT

victims or beings who are "toyed with" ... there is absolutely nothing to be afraid of, to feel

powerless about in all of this. We are, each and every human and plant and animal and every

other lifeform in this Universe, CHOOSING with God what form(s) we wish to inhabit, to explore

the myriad and yes, Infinite environments, that exist in the Universes. We Choose which

vessel to inhabit and experience in... we are, each of us, intimately involved in the Creation of

our own Unique Sacred Vessel(s). Will it be a Light Body, incandescent and radiant and

without high densities; will it be a heavy duty Earth bound vessel made up of a "physical,

mental, emotional" and ultimately Soul-based frequencies? What we choose to experience,

what we choose to explore is 100% our own free will choice. This is true for every living thing.

The "issues" arise when we become in a state of feeling separate from the Love that Co-

Created our unique vessel... i.e., when through free will choices, we choose to explore what it

is like to "Not Feel Love." For, this IS a choice. None of us, animal, or human or Nature or

Earth or Beyond, is a "victim" ... we just forget We ARE LOVE, that's all! But then, there are

so many guides, and helpers, Angels, entities,... you name it, Thousands and Thousands of beings and Beings of many varied frequencies offering their help to us, to help us "Remember The Love" ...

Earth Changes and the whole 2012 matrix of "Waking Up" and moving on up the frequencies from deep densities of emotionally entangled despair, powerlessness, hopelessness, anger, rage, .. all of these emotions that we developed while exploring in our uniquely designed and Co-Created body! Sacred Body! We have chosen these energies, to experience them, to experience what it is like to forget we Are Love, to experience and make free will choices (that create Karma) based on feeling Loveless in our Ego Universe.

But it is all a dream, and we are all Waking Up! It is time to go Home to the Heart! It is OK to feel the Love again – to Feel the Love Prior to this dense, shutdown ego based hall of fear-filled mirrors. For that is what it is, a dream, a self-created hall of mirrors, based on feeling all alone, all separated from the Truth of What We Are.

And this is OK! So we chose to go through this! Why? I do not "know" but LOVE LOVES and God LOVES That Is All There IS   LOVE!   So if I am going to ask a question, it might be, how will I relate to this astoundingly beautiful unique form I have Co-Created with the Sacred Body Factories today? In this Moment? How will I relate to my emotions, my body, my mind, my Soul and all its truly marvelous, astoundingly amazingly beautiful Creations that I AM?!!

There are, as I have said, many levels of the Sacred Body Factories and there will be more on this in this present book you are holding in your Sacred Hand, and in other books to come.

Please, Love Yourself Love YourSelf Turn To the Love You Are NOW and allow all the beings who are trying to help you Wake Up! Help you! Allow yourself to Receive the Love You Are. For this is the Truth.   The hall of mirrors of separation that we have all chosen to explore is but a dream, ending for those of us who wish to give up this sense of separation and all its agonal lies. LOVE LOVES This IS All.   There Is Only Love.   I Love You.   Shoh Nah Hah Lieh

The Sacred Body Factories

THIS IS A TRUE DREAM

I am here, resting in the radiant Gold Light, Gold all around and within Everything in this Space. The many Rainbows of Infinite Hew riding above us, singing in Colors imaginable to us all if we would but Remember.

The Golden Light, the suffusion of all Here with this Light as we all tend to the torsos in front of us; which like dressmakers' models, but of fleshyLight, are in a single line from one side of Infinity to the other, across this Divine Factory within which we are Creating.

I am slightly bent over, carefully checking the Solar Plexus technologies of Light, of Divine Love, that reside, spontaneously within the created torso on its stand.   So erect, so..yes, it must be said, so "solidly in place," so appropriately in place in this infinite lineup of torso offerings, creations for the Souls to Manifest and Explore and become deeply identified with during coming incarnations in the Ego Field.

I look up from my Loving, relaxed, Surrendered work, Up, high above us in the Golden Light which Radiantly imbues and engenders us all... The Forest of Light The Trees of Light The Torsos of Light... Up Up to there high high above us, where literally thousands of beings, laughing, jesting, jostling, Ecstatically wait for their Divine Vessel to be Created, to be made

Uniquely for each of these Souls, so they may explore, navigate, be part of the Experiments which are so self Willingly, so Soul Willingly, manifested within the Ego Field.

The feeling beneath my fingers of the fleshy- Light Solar Plexus workings, the Solar Plexus requirements, technically aligned with the Divine Emotional, Mental, Physical... All must be extremely accurate, precise, Lovingly aligned to what each Soul needs for its Journey through the Ego Field which is this Universe we have chosen to reside in; and its return Home when its Unique exploration is done for this round... "what encasement," "what frequency bands," "what,...?" data collected yet again for Divine Union and Sharing.

And who/what is "collecting" all this data? For it has to be being collected in order to make the Next Divine Vessel for the Next Divine Incarnation of that Happy, Ecstatic, awaiting Soul... there, high high above me. The absolute JOY that is within these Souls at the Feeling they will be actually exploring within this Ego field that has been created for this particular kind of Evolution.. The total Ecstacy I Feel in my Heart, my Golden Heart, my Heart aligned Uniquely to the Love That Lives Us All.

Aligned to the Love that IS this Divine Vessel I am working on, this Divine Solar Plexus energetic frequency radiant bands of Love, of True Life, that will Clothe, Nourish, Protect, LOVE the Soul on its Journeys "There and Back" Over and Over and Over The countless Comings and Goings Comings and Goings...

The Falling into the Ego field, the agreed to "forgetting" what We Truly Are. The identification with the separation we feel so deeply, so traumatically inside this Divine Vessel... the creation of ego, of feeling being separate from What We Really Are : Love...

Each Soul, clothed in its Rainment of Light, of Divine Love, falls falls down down down the Manifestation Chambers, step by step the frequencies are lowered and lowered and lowered until the accommodative frequencies are reached whereby the Soul-Body connection can be felt, lived in, nurtured, in its chosen dense environments. Evolving once again, one more "lifetime," one more incarnation, one more manifestation... as "me being my body mind" as me "separate from Feeling Love" as me, human, animal, plant, rock, other... forgetting that I am separate from the Love I Am. Forgetting everything

So that the Divine Vessel I inhabit now, my Soul inhabits now energetically, can do its evolution in the unique manner of this Universe it now inhabits, this Universe of Polarities, of Dualities, of feeling all alone in the Divine Casing it has Chosen to explore in...

And so we have evolved, let's say Darwinianly, for someone had to figure it out here, within the separative lives we all live, based on deep fear that resides within the profound vulnerability of the all alone body mind emotional field we each have chosen to inhabit...

Oh, how the identification of "me" with my body, my mind, my emotions as generated from the feelings of being separate, from being all alone within my "skin" ... Oh, how well has this experiment "worked" !! But this is another story for another time...

I look up, and as I do so, I am wondering Who/What is working on the head, the face, the brain? Who is working on the front limbs, the hind limbs, the fins, the long sensitive tails, the wings... while in front of me and in the infinite line of torsos from horizon to horizon in this Golden Forest of Light... encased, the neck, the heart, the solar plexus and all its organs, the generative organs, the root - this last, the impulse to LIVE to stay Alive AS the body! Yes, I work on these too, I can feel and Feel I do work on these too.

There are so many levels of experience, of existence... for even as I am working on this particular torso, I am also navigating as are you, and you, and you, this Divine Ego Field... And part of this Divine Experiment in what does it Feel like to Not Feel the Love I Am... oh, how brutal it has been! How brutal it is!! And yet, wonder! the simultaneity of our Existences!!

But then, in the midst of all the forgetting : I Remember : I chose. And from this choice, living in this Divine Vessel created for my needs as a Soul within the Sacred Body Factories... I am choosing I will choose What a profound and Gifted Life this is! To Feel Beyond the Ego Field to so many other ways of Manifesting as a Soul; and yet, simultaneously to feel the "stuckness" within the Ego Field... mired within the karma I have created in the deep belief that I am a separate all alone being unLoved.... But of course it is a lie, a huge part of me knows, feels and Feels it is a lie!

And thus does evolution of this Darwinian sort, based in root fear ... ultimately evolving experiencially and energetically into true Evolution... but it all happened the way it happened. How powerful I am to have created so much agony in my life as separate from the Love I Am, in these limited, and particularly intense Soul's experiences! I find I am laughing! It is so absurd! But IT FEELS SO REAL! And yet my Soul Feels it is Not Real, and my Soul I need to attend to more truthfully, more trustingly, more Lovingly. No more abandonment of the Gifts.

Which, as I am working on my own Solar Plexus issues in the Sacred Body Factory, as well as on the many other Souls' Solar Plexus needs in the Sacred Body Factories, and on the egoically created fear based solar plexus issues in the ego field... Oh My God... and then there is the DreamTime!

But that is another story, for another time... this life for sure, but for now... For Now this Moment Divine :

My Prayer   Thank You God for this Life, for this Divine Moment, for Your Never Ending Love Help me to Be Love and Its Expression Now and in Every Moment Divine!   Thank You God

Many As One

As I rest in this space creating for the Sacred Body Factories, a hundred starlings appear,

rising and falling in the sky of Earth outside my window, the whirrrrr of their wings as they

move as one huge expression, Being, to and from the field outside my house... the shared

movement, the many as one of them   Unseen between each a signal, a psychic chord is struck

telling each what the perceived "other" is "going to do" and then, as one, All Move! How is this

possible? What is the wonderful Living energy between each in the All of this brown winged

mass of many as one?

And what is the Living Energy between each in the All of this Ego Field we inhabit, the

sharing of frequency bands that enable us to "know" before we know in the mind.. that enables

us to "feel" in the body, in the emotional field, what the perceived "other" will do, is up to?

The psychic energies that lie between each and every one of us is observable on a daily basis...

the Sacred Body, and Its Sacred Node which so Lovingly holds and caretakes the Sacred Body

"Knows" and more importantly "Feels" the consequences of the shared harmonically

resonating frequencies.

It Lives By this

We Live By This

Harmonically Shared Breath Feeling Knowing Intuiting Seeing Smelling Hearing Tasting

Touching Within/Without all the same actually...

This place has been called a resonating hall of mirrors in one sense, yes? Who am I really?

How much of "me" is truly independent of each and every other resonating perceived "other" in

this Ego field? How much of "me" is without the Breath of the Beloved Living me? How much

of each of us is without the Breath of Life? Shared Felt Resonating between us and

supporting us and helping us to keep "feeling alive" in this far away, shut down, darkened

space of separateness from God, the Love We Truly Are? Love, self Love - for each "self"

has its own Unique frequency bands of Love, of Source, unlike any other in the Universes.

The Breath of Many is the Breath of One It can be no other way, the Sacred Bodies

resting and Receiving resting and Giving Back... seeking, actively yearning for more and more

stimulating experiences... yearning, and yet contracting away from the Beloved...

How Conscious is any of it? This has become one of the most important issues... How

Conscious am I How Conscious are you, my "perceived other" with regard to the Breath, the

Shared Harmonically Resonating Being(s) that We Are One Huge Resonating Field of each

Uniquely Resonating Frequency Bands...

As the Starlings in Flight As the Starlings in mutual spontaneous Breath and Movement,

Instantaneously Bonded... by what? But Bonded each one is, there is no doubt of this. How fortunate we are to be living now, alive now within this Ego Field that is Growing and Evolving ever more deeply and profoundly to the Joy We Are!   What a gift we have been Given.   Have always been Given. Yes, Consciousness, and the Conscious clarification of all that blocks the Pure Breath, the Beloved, from Living us, from Living the Sacred Body, the Sacred Node...

All is in place for us, in this very moment. Come, let us Begin, a New Moment, a New Breath, a New Spark, a New Radiance of each of us Uniquely foreverNow

Spontaneous : It comes into me, into my heart and mind to recall, now that the starlings have left to play elsewhere on the Earth... how long did it take for each unit, each being, each particle of Life that is a unique arising here, a Unique Arising of God, each Starling IS a Unique Arising of God, of the Beloved..

How long did it "really take" for the "perceived one" starling to "neurologicallybodidly" grasp and respond to the signal, to the shared signal to rise to fall to swirl to inundate as One, as "a group"...   much much less than a second of our human mentally ticking "time"...

And, what Is an Instant   what Is Spontaneous   What Is the Sacred Breath of Many As One NOW?

Amen and Thank You God for these days of Joyous Loving Relationship with You with the Breath of You with your Love with Your Infinite Creations as forms arising, falling, swirling, dancing, singing, . . . Coming and Going   Coming and Going   Ever Transforming Ever

Renewed   Forever

              Now

                     Always

Picture A Membrane

Picture a membrane, a membrane of Light and Light-as-Matter: Studded membrane with globules of evenaesant Light of varying frequencies... from the most dense to the more delicate, even insubstantial... But all required for the "passing over" for the Transition from the Ego Field densities (frequencies) into the higher frequencies of Life that lie beyond . . .

Let's call it a "Transition Chamber" this globule, this Resting place, this Vessel of Transformation into higher Realms of our Existences; a Vessel of Change Charged with Love, packed with iridescent Holographic Pixels of Love which help the Soul aspect which is dropping Its Sacred Body to accommodate ItSelf once again to Higher Frequencies. Within this Chamber of Loving Change are All the Resources the Soul aspect needs to Remember Its lives inhabiting Sacred Bodies thru the millennia; All the Resources the Soul aspect needs to Remember the Love it Is... A recuperative Globe of Divine energies CoCreated with God, with the Love We All Are.

These Chambers of Transition and Transformation stud the resonating band that has come to be known as the Ego Veil, which in fact is not really a "veil" but specifically resonating bands of Light interacting in such a manner as to create the sense/feeling of separation from what is Prior to this band. It is not that we are REALLY separate, but that we are choosing to explore with profound Light Technologies what it is "like to feel separate." This "Ego Veil" is a

Creation of the Sacred Body Factories and Beyond to help the Souls who yearn for such

experiences as separation from Love and what "happens"!!   Ohhhhh, yes, we ALL Choose!!

And so, too, these Chambers of Transition and Transformation which stud the "Ego Veil"

which is our particular Universe's "boundaries," are available to the Soul aspects yearning to

once again inhabit the Sacred Bodies available to them on behalf of the Sacred Body Factories,

on behalf of their own blessings in Free Will and CoCreation with the Sacred Body Factories.

Nothing we do, or Create, or are, or Manifest, or de-Manifest, or Transform, or drop, or end,

or begin with, or leave...   Nothing is not "known" to our Soul of these journeys.   However the

given Soul aspect will be infused with informations from many levels to ensure its lack of

Remembering/Feeling Love while falling deeply asleep Into the Ego Field, our special, unique,

and truly profound Universe. And also built into the specific Soul aspect are triggers for

Remembering, for Feeling Again, When The Time Is Right and above all else, when the Soul

aspect Chooses to Remember, to Feel Again. Much of the Creation in the Sacred Body

Factories is to aid in the "Forgetting" and to aid in the "Remembrance" on the part of the

Soul aspect.   So much of these Journeys are again, a matter of becoming more Conscious,

Remembering how Creative We Are   yes, Remembering

And Now, let's visit these wondrous Chambers of Change, of Transformation, ultimately, of

Ascension of our Realm also :

The first thing we notice is that we recognize everything. We recognize the beings who await us. We recognize the Sacred Body Factories' personnel. We recognize "who/what" we Are! We become Consciously Responsible in our Remembrance... these Chambers are Loving Opportunities to become more fully Conscious of What/Who We Really Are... but like everything in Evolution it is a stepwise Process : The memories are stepwisely given back You will get what you are able to accommodate... and what you are able to accommodate is your Choice, your Free Will. It is NOT about forced Remembrance. Those cruel experiments have ended - not exactly "failed experiments" but certainly not experiments founded in Love. Even in the Evolution of the Universes there is Evolution ever more deeply into Love, to Feeling and Remembering Who We Are.

All is done gently here, within these Chambers of Loving Change. Where fear arises, and it will, for the Soul aspect is still soaked in its Karmic residues... in all its informations gathered for the Great Experiment of What is it like to forget the Love You Are... What is it like to Feel No Love... What is it like to be imprisoned within ego structures based in feeling you are unloved, undeserving, unwanted, abandoned by the Great Love, the Beloved?... Cruel, yes, it can be interpreted as such. But each and every Soul and all its Soul aspects choose willingly, with Free Will, and yes, great Excitement and Happiness, to explore from this state of Lovelessness. Oh, this Great Experiment, which has been so profoundly successful. We all believe we are the ego. It has worked tremendously well!

But it is time to Remember : To return while either still in our Divine Bodies or out of our

Divine Bodies, to the Love We Are, Prior to ego, to separation from our own True Selves.

These Transition Chambers provide the means for Awakening if we so choose, and in the past

especially for those who have left the Divine Body or who have chosen once again to inhabit a

Divine Body provides all the support, guidance, informations as needed.   And Now, with the

Ascension Process, in each Moment, in the Now, we can access these Chambers of Loving Life

in the Now while still inhabiting our Divine Bodies. While still on Planet Earth and truly well and

deep within the Ego Field, which by its Own Free Will is being blasted Lovingly Consciously by

the Light, by the Universal Love ever more deeply and profoundly in these Earth Changes. All is

available now   Now   Nothing is hidden anymore. It is just an issue of How Conscious do I want

to Be, to Become? How much do I want to Be Loving, BeThe Love I Am Now? In this moment,

and in this one, and in this one...?   All will be Given that is needed,

 And,

We remember it all   We Remember It All   Because We Created It All

Amen

Dear Creature, When I look at you...

Dear Creature, when I look at you, feel you, all I can feel is wonder - What are you? Really?

Who are you really?   You have a distinctive grace as you trot down the path before me.   You

have wonderful movement and line when you roll about on the new green grasses, or at my feet

in the kitchen on the blue and white tile floor.   You create the most amazing sound in your

flying overhead, over my roof swooping so low I am sure you will take my roof with you.   You

rise up and you come down. You turn so magnificently within some Feeling of yourself, your

unique presentation here, on this dear Mother Earth.

Who are you dear friend who has been in my heart long before I can remember with my

human brain? What are you that I have felt you soft and tugging and warm enough to curl up

next to and sleep for 1,000 years? Where have you been?   Where are you going?   Touch

Smell See you but never measure you, no, never measure you again.

Thank you for being and for being here, with me, on this journey, in this exploration of the

Cosmos that we share, that we are One of.

I will write you more tomorrow, I promise this dear friend in my heart Opening to the Love

That Lives Us All.   And let us share again in the dream time in the moment of memory, and

Now, in this moment of Creation. I Love you dear friend.   Good night.

What amazes me a lot...

Dear Friend: What amazes me a lot is that my dreamtime with you is the same now as the so-called awake time.   There is only one of us as we pad on thickened feet through the marshes and tall grasses.   There is only one of us as we squawk our warning through the evening air at the movement passing us,...there...then moving on, relax.   There is only one of us lifting off softly from the flower nectar sticky to the long mouth of us   a crater of yellow and red and green opening beneath us

There is only one of us the night sky swirling the comet billowing stars the wind moving through our body   the drop to earth is soft the blade of grass the scinter of glassy stone the wealth of wateriness descending with us   To land to float to rest to return

When we fell together...

When we fell together into this field of closed off memories such wrenching pain agony of not

Remembering together occlusions abound the webbing matrices entrench our Souls cries our

grief our not Remembering our own death from Who We Are call call to each other over the

reefs the oceans of not Remembering the cells curl in on themselves in foetal birthing into this

new realm of darkened Light Trundled Bundled Rippling choices surrendered to the coming

into this realm Heart Beating Heart Beating Breath taken Breath received Breath given

Breathe Breathe our way beneath the Falling Light the not Remembering Guides us back home

It is a gift to know you...

It is a gift to know you   It is a gift to share this realm with you, your uniqueness arising from

the Source of What Lives Us All   Even as one is birthed   Breathed   Birthed   Never Ending

but, Oh, How I become enamored of your unique casing, the body, the beauty of its lines, its

carrying of itself in this Gravity.   What a wonder you are, there is nothing like you anywhere

else in this Universe of Light and Sound and wonder!

This encasing that we share   this feeling so shut off from... from...   What?   Do you know, I

don't even know what I feel shut off from?   A wandering about of the mind   a forgetting of the

heart   a taking for granted of the breath...

I long to keep you forever   no, not exactly as you are   but as what I need you to be, for me,

to help me feel safe here   to help me feel and know myself   to help me one day learn to birth

myself anew in each microsecond of Feeling You.   How wonderful you are to abide me, to help

me learn to abide myself.

And truly, how very wonderful that abiding can become Love.

The gusto the greed the need with which...

The gusto the greed the need with which we attack the food   Set down before us with hands

that know the love of preparation -   How our need creates ignorance the closed off spaces,

that chaos within. . .   mouth filling tongue too longing for even taste throat closed off tightly

before / after each ravenous gulp.   Where is the longing to Relate to this Offering? Who

told us we were not allowed to receive and feel what we receive in the Loving arisings of this

preparation, this creation?   Who are we this body that lies and rests upon the floor our face

stuck within the nurturing vessel?   What is this body that has forgotten the caressing of the

side of the dish with a tongue attuned to the Love of what Truly Feeds the bodymind, the

bodyemotions?   Where have we gone in this kitchen of the Soul that has walled about it a

desperate sense of starvation wherever it turns, whatever new earthly environment it inhabits?

Well, dear friend, no matter.   For there is always enough, no matter the cellular memories

which have aligned themselves to a feelingbelief there is never enough - "Never Enough!!"

gonging within our forgetting terror-filled existence here.

There was a man named Darwin who captured well enough this sense of limited resources, of

there never being enough.   Who made it a measureable creed, making possible assessment of

the world through our fear   Who, while we remain within these walls of this unFeeling kitchen, will be a kind of god to us, and who truly was mistaken.   For there is always enough, no matter

the forgetting...

It would perhaps be good to study the feeling of "enough" in and of itself, to learn to slow

down and Feel Beyond "enough" to That which Hovers in the air about the bowl within which our

snout rests, and Streams through the windows quaking and shaking this house. That which

Allows an expansion beyond the fear that creates this Un-real contracted environment of that

lie: "never enough"

The calling of the Source of All resources arises and hammers at our door in every moment.

God walks through our house and into the kitchen stands over us and smiles and lays down next

to us   Its Multitudes Arising From Its Hands In Loving Presentation   strokes the weary

fearfilled body, softening the resistance to truly Receiving Food   to Feeling Food,...the Love

of self, the Love of the True Self once again Felt.   Our head rests in the bowl, satiated.

Meditation with the Cows...

THIS IS A TRUE STORY

For as long as I have lived here in this place, 20 years or so, down the road from me there is a

farmer I do not know his name, who, every year brings in a new herd of cows - and of course

every year the yearling herd go to market.   These cows, or it would be more accurate to call

them steer as they are always male, have, since they began to come onto his farm feel very

close to me.   I do not know why.   It is just this happy feeling I get whenever I drive by and I

see the herd in its place, doing what they do, being what they are, they never seem to question

Now, as the years have gone by, more and more there is what feels like true relationship

developing between myself and my friends. And sometimes I will stop right beside them in my

car as their yard is close to the road, with the big old barn and the fields and their human's

home right there.   The road is a busy road.   It is called Dexter – Chelsea road.

I have noticed, over these years, how my being more and more a space of opening to my

feelings again, with the opening of my shut-down heart again, that my relationship to these

friends who are giving their bodies so that humans my live, has changed and changed.   I

especially want to tell you about tonight, on the way home from Meditation, what happened that

has never ever happened before - even though I have called to them, stopped my car, and

waited before...

Tonight, as I was driving through the villages near where I live, a voice said quite lovely, "Go see the cows" ...and this wonderful feeling/Feeling of God and Love which I was still carrying and holding and being became even deeper.   I followed this voice, and turned onto Dexter-Chelsea road. I drove gently the miles to where my friends the cows live.   It was still light outside, and I could see the young males, about one dozen of them in the nearest field.   I stopped the car beside them.   I was filled with Love for them, with a feeling of GOD, and I called out to them,   "Hello! Hello! I Love You, I Love You, my friends,..."   I was so Happy!

And lo and behold, two of these beauties broke from the herd and came hop skipping jumping their tails twisting and waggling and ran to the fence! And then, one by one, or in twos and threes the others came scampering, kicking their heels, waggling their tails, swinging their heads, jumping towards the fence.   It was Incredibly Beautiful! They were Deeply In Love With Me. And I was Deeply In Love With Them...   I could feel/Feel it profoundly in my body.

And I talked to them about God, and about Love, and I told them that they never ever had to do this again if they did not want to,...   that they were already Free to make a choice about their bodies...   that there was Only Love, self/Self Loving First

Each and every one stood there, extremely still, very attentive, and Meditated with me, and held the Space of God and Shared their Love of God of this Planet of their Hearts for all of us. It was a very very moving experience.   I do not know how to describe it, but I wanted so much to tell you all about it! They were consciously choosing to come toward me/Me... toward the

Meditation, toward the Radiance of the One That Lives Us All, GOD.   They were pressing on

the fence, so still, so attentive.

Many cars went by, some slowing down to see what was going on. And it became necessary for

me to move, as the friends were pressing, pressing against the fence, and it was not a strong

fence by any means.   I sang that There Is Only Love   I blew them many kisses   I promised that

I would be back to see them all again, to Meditate with them again,   Yes...   I feel so very

Blessed by all of it.   Thank you for your time with sharing. I Love You.

"If you do not Love yourself you cannot Love the Universe" [1]

"If you do not Love yourself you cannot Love the Universe" How this resounds in our Soul,

beloved. Where did we lose track of who we Really Are, you, me, One? Where did we step off

into the blankness numbness frozen states we now share, one in this apparent togetherness?

Oh GOD Why have you forsaken me!? HAVE YOU forsaken me? Where are you the Joy

Ecstasy Bliss Breath of Heaven in our excruciating resistant physical lungs? How did this

happen? How could we possibly choose such a dumbeddown un-Feeling existence? DID I

CHOOSE THIS?!! What is Evolution anyway?

And so the brain chatters away, chomping on bits of flying moods and emotions that keep

arising in our field... What are we running away from? Why do we not want to feel how we

truly feel in these moods that remorselessly run us, that we constantly try to escape? What is

so hateful and fearfilling about our moods, about how we feel in these fields that continue to

arise, that we try endlessly to wrap our thoughtforms around to explain, explain, explain...?

Or, that we shove down, down, down into forgetfulness? That resonating, ever present

pressure unconsciousness? A kind of gravity. . .

And now, Dear Animal Friend, we can feel, can we not, how you do not particularly share or

participate in this need for "explaining" whatever arises, yes? How you are not so heavily

invested in turning aside from these uncomfortable feelings that arise and become, for us, an identity, a prison, an image - a self - a never ending dance to stay the same, the same self

seeking verification of its existence in constantly changing environments, with constantly

changing stimuli.

How is it we have become trapped within the apparent never ending field of arisings?   A self

alone and separate with deep drive to remain separate inside its own skin?

So, what is preventing us, dear beloved One of my Heart Opening to What Lives Us All simply

stepping outside this... over and over? This returning to rectify to clarify to purify to jump in

again, all over!?...   Why keep coming back anyway!?

Why not just step outside here for a breather, for a re-Union with the Beloved? For has not

the Beloved Always Forever and Ever just Been Here?   Where are we looking anyway? Why

are we always "looking," there, a hand above the eyebrows shading the Light so we can see

better into the hazy murky inundating never-ending arisings here?

For It Is already here, now anyway. What's the battle? The Love does not turn away from us,

we turn away from the Love;   and, "In any case, all beings are Loved by the Universe,

Utterly." [2]

[1,2]Title and last line from Michael Innocence's works, as yet unpublished

Hello dear friend   There you are....

THIS IS A TRUE STORY

Hello dear friend   There you are lying in the overhanging shade from the garage roof, drowsy

happy in this heat of noon.   I pick you up, an apparent separate form from me, in apparent

separate bodyemotionmind format from me, and hold you tightly as the warmth for the body is

so deep today, this wondrous moment of loving you dear friend.   Softly.   Purring gently snoozy

caress in happiness just to have you here with me.   The Light shared in this sense of bodily

oneness.   Merging and so I look down to where you had lain before in the sense of your bodily

surrender to the dear Mother, Earth, your long softfurred body relaxed in a way that if I would

I could feel envious!   And there lies the Butterfly.   It is still alive still wavering gently its torn

wings longing for the flight into the still Light which surrounds us here, now;   perhaps longing

for the stillness of its own form in the merging with the Love Living It, That Lives Us All.

Perhaps, steeped, in an effort to remain within this lovely battered form dusty wings almost

colorless from the brilliant once Monarch Orange White Black hues.

I pick you up and spread open the wings of Love to the Light which Breathes down so brilliantly

from the sky of Earth, from the Sun of this Planet who helped form your loveliness.   I gently

hold your wings open to this Light and your little long proboscis seeks   seeks   the moisture of some flower perhaps,   tapping tapping its tip along my palm fluttering seeking mouth   perhaps longing for nector, perhaps the long flight Home so short now?

I place you among the honeysuckle in such a way that you will not fall and within the bright Light of day you settle within these Cherished Blossom of God of Love for you and suckle and die your body's death your form's ending as a separate expression here, as an apparent separate arising here, in these realms that feel each of us so far away from Home.   In this moment, Merged, and so,

I return to kitty purring and rolling in the soft sand of the drive. His beauteous body of Light of God reflected here within these realms that feel so far from Home.   I pick you up.   I hold my self within my arms dear Butterfly dear One furry within the realms of Love Here Now This Moment   We are Home   All One again

God Bless you dearest Heart in my human breast for helping me to Feel again this acceptance to the Birthing of All Things which resides Within this Union with God   that can Be, Truly, yes, Truly Felt Here, Now

No longer the need to seek within the forms arising here, for succor, for sustenance, for space, for safety, for protection, oh Vulnerable quaking child's heart be still

Safe

And so I yield.   I Surrender.   I submit my whole being and my whole Being to You.   And I

Merge with the All that Arises in apparent separateness from You.

Oh, Form divine.

    Oh, Butterfly.

        Oh, kitty.

            Oh, myself.   Oh, LightLoveHappiness Expressed Now.

And Now.

Forever Now.

Amen

The Node as Template

There have been different experiments in what can be called "Nodal accommodation of the Soul" via the Sacred Body; this has resulted in the following areas of exploration :

The Node as Template

The Sacred Body as Template

The Soul as Template

The relationship between these, in the existence of a Being, in the actual manifestation and incarnation of the Soul, is accommodated through the layering of interconnected frequency bands that harmonically align themselves to embedded (pre-existing, pre-created) frequency bands of the Template (FB-T).

Thus there are, in effect, layered Templates, tucked one within the other like the lovely Russian dolls and Easter eggs - the interconnecting frequency bands, at this level known as chords, nadis, meridians... but which, with each "ascending" Template of frequency bands becomes less and less dense, more and more refined higher frequencies, but which Penetrate All the Layers of All the Templates ultimately at all levels of Creation.

I have heard it said, at least 200 times here, that Earth Plane matter is the "most dense" - i.e., the slowest, most dense frequency bands of which the Template is partially comprised.

The Sacred Body is designed to exist in the relatively narrow and designated Earth Matter

densities, and thus the Soul aspect in its "descent" into matter via the Manifestation Chambers

of our Universe, of our Ego Field, accommodates itself to ever increasing forces of compaction,

of contraction, step by step increasing its density-expression to be able to "live in, inhabit, have

as template here" the Sacred Body. A Sacred Vessel that feels itself separate from the Love

that has in fact CoCreated it in one of infinite manifested "forms" of Divine Love. In fact one

of the ultimate expressions of this Divine Love : Human, Animal, Plant, Rock, Crystal, Water,

Sky, Volcano, Earth Earth Earth Home to the multitudes of intersecting harmonically

resonating Template fields.

Each Soul has chosen to do this, to experience this compression, this contraction, this descent

into the Ego Field and all the wondrous opportunities for exploration, for expression and for

evolution offered while in this state of feeling separate from What Created It, What Lives It.

Has Always Lived It   Love

*   *   *   *   *   *   *

There is, built into the Sacred Body Template all the Stages of the "development" of the Soul

aspect's manifestation from egg + sperm to embryo to fetus to infant to adult. The body has

built into it with profoundly Loving and high Light technological skill the Soul's necessary

Template, by Contract, by Free Will Contract, all that is needed to navigate and explore and evolve as an experimental lifeform within this Ego field. Genetics is one aspect of this built in technology and has had contributions to it from many "off Planet" lifeforms.

The Soul, in agreement, in Free Will, "signs the Contract" and is actively involved in the Creation in the Sacred Body Factories of the Sacred Body Templates with which Its many aspects will navigate the Realm that Earth Herself is navigating and exploring and growing and evolving within. For She is a Living Being as are all Planetary Bodies, Stars, Nebulae,... all are lifeforms with their own Sacred Templates CoCreated with the Divine.

In our case, here on Earth, the preprogramming of the Body's relationship to the Nodal Template is partial - Evolution in the sense of Darwinian evolution of the species, the various Nodal contributions embedded within the sense of Time/Space in our Universe could not occur otherwise. More will be discussed on this at another time.

The Potential, or latent possibilities which reside in the Templates of the Body-Node and within the Node-Body is preprogrammed entirely. Otherwise the Body-Node could not survive – i.e., could not retain its integrity within - the limited parameters (the Paradigm) of the Ego Field. Within and between these limits and the Potential is "evolution" as we have come to experience it, to know it; Darwinian evolution based in the alienation from Feeling What Lives Us. However, with the ongoing Ascension Process, new aspects of Nodal-Body interface are constantly being "upgraded" with ever increasing finer and finer frequencies WITHIN the Node

WITHIN the Body - truly a profoundly Sacred Journey, Experiment, ... Spiritual Evolution now rapidly underway here! Awakening Remembering here, now, each embodied within the Sacred Vessel on Earth...

How the frequency bands are shared between the individual, the groups, the species, the Kingdoms, the Earth, the Sun & Moon, the Planets, our Galaxy, all the Galaxies, our Universe, and Beyond Our Universe... All are founded on Harmonically Resonating Fields of shared frequencies; more or less consciously, and unconsciously shared by each and every living entity in our Universe and Beyond.

The Breath

Inside the Sacred Node, suspended within the Ego Field with billions, trillions of other Sacred Nodes, harmonically resonating between and within each and "perceived other" the Breath prevails   The Breath IS   The Breath required for continued existence, continued manifestation, continued exploration of the Ego field.   The Breath, what Is It?

You will notice that to breathe is involuntary, that to breathe is a basic requirement for all life here, the movement of the gills, the movement of the lungs, the movement of the chloroplast membranes, the exchange of life giving Oxygen for CO_2 for us, the exchange of life giving CO_2 for Oxygen in plants. . .   Everything here that lives depends upon the exchanges that occur in Life Giving Breath, over which we have no "control" except to "hold the breath" for a time, but not too long a time... we cannot...not too long for the Bursting Forth of the held unReceiving breath will make room within us for the New Breath,   the absolutely required Breath of Life. The Earth too Breathes and this needs to be Felt, Remembered.   There is no existence on this Planet but that it Breathes.

Within the Sacred Body there is an area of the brain which has been designed to Breathe, which Receives the Radiance of the Light of God, the Radiance of the Love That Is this Cosmos, that Loves each and every one of us. And ultimately as we evolve, the whole Sacred Body Breathes; for when we breathe physically, we are actually Breathing in the Love of God, into our brain, into our Sacred Vessels. With every breath/Breath this is true. It is a matter of becoming ever more Conscious of this, of developing a Loving Feeling Relationship to the Breath that is our Beloved Birthright. For every being here by Divine Right deserves to Breathe, to Live, to Manifest. And this is true in all the Universes.

The subject of the Breath, of Its ultimately Divine Origen has been discussed by many Teachers, written of in many books for millennia. It is not a new concept. But the Feeling Relationship to the Breath, the becoming Conscious of this Feeling Relationship to the Breath, to Feel it penetrate the Sacred Body, the Node, the Earth, the Ego Field our Universe... This is now becoming available to us more and more Consciously, to explore, to share, to experience in a manner of great ease now for all of us... As the fear, the protection of our vulnerabilities, our contraction away from the Universe's Gifts recede, so do we Open Open Breathe Breathe Love more deeply, more Consciously and, ultimately, in any case, Love IS Consciousness.

The Breath of the Sacred Node, of the Sacred Body which is housed within the Sacred Node is but one expression of the Divine Living us in every moment. The Breath of the Nodes, suspended within the Ego Field, the Sacred Breath Shared by Harmonic Resonance among all suspended Blessed Caretakers of the Sacred Bodies.

The connection between the Feeling Hearts of Sacred Bodies, Hearts of Sacred Nodes, Hearts of Great Planets, Hearts of Great Suns, Hearts of the Center of our Galaxy, of Hearts of the

Centers of All Great Galaxies within our Universe extending to All Hearts of All Universes

Infinitely... The Sacred Breath connects All to All How could it be otherwise, for there is no

separation, just an experiment we have chosen to create ourselves into, to feel what it is like

to not Share the Sacred Breath; it is, certainly, a kind of hell. But for those of us who so

choose, this experience as hell ends. Yes.

There Is Light In This Offering . . .

There is Light in this Offering, in this body, in these body parts you have sacrificed up at your

body's slaughter. I can feel, now within my own body, my physicalness, here, the shared

offering that I am consuming, . .

Light as Meat.   No, do not ride lightly, easily over this, avoiding the emotional forays into the

predator field you have carried for millennia, since the beginning of "eating" "consuming" . . .

The levels of consciousness of the body parts and beings we are partaking of, the feeling of

saliva drool the throat opening to receive slewed off portions of the body part the stomach

receiving after involuntary contractile passage down the slippery esophageal channel the

acids...

How remarkable it is that chemistries have been created that dissolve these offerings that my

own bodyemotionmind may continue here...   How much Light IS there in this Offering? How

much Manifested GOD is actually contained within the cellular structures of these Meditated

cows, my dear friends for years on my trips home from work, from meditation, from meetings,

from visits with clients, from shopping?

My dear friends, the Cows : Cells shining Radiantly with the Light Shared between us in deep

and JoyFilled Meditations, their calf gamboling and tail swinging leaping about filling the field

with their bellowing and carrying on   YOUNG CALF   YOUNG ONES   in my heart

Swelling to adolescence, and still gamboling, meditating, carrying forth the wonders of this

Planet within your own growths, . .

GROW,   FILL WITH THE LIGHT my dear friends . .

Shared bodies   Light filled cells   Innundated mysteries of our lives here, on this wondrous

Planet, Earth   CONSUMED BY THE LIGHT   All are ultimately consumed by the Light :

Beloved of the Light Which Births Us All . . .

And yet, dear friends, who has ordained the mindless, unfeeling pressing forward into the 18

Wheeler? Why have you agreed to such monstrously inhumane treatment of your Divine Body?

Separation bodily from friends, carted down highways congested with unfeeling

bodymindshearts streaming past you in contracted, unfeeling vehicular insulations?   Thank GOD

for what I need to feel as a moment of your forgetting, your "unconsciousness"   -   Is this

what I need to help me blank out yet again what I have seen with my own eyes, felt in my own

body, that you are going through, that you are going to go through, have gone through, in your

provisioning, your gifting, your sacrifice?

You are my friends.   I remember each and every one of you over years providing me with

necessary slowing down and Feeling - FEELING the Oneness that We Already Are. Feeling

the apparent separation of our bodies as you gaze at me, playfully, galavanting about these

Shared Fields of Light : I sit in my car and I hold this Space of Feeling and I Allow myself to

Feel you in my Body Shared As OneLightLoveGOD. . .   And I Pray:

Oh GOD help me to heal this pain of this untrue separation of my Beloved from me   Help me to

Feel GOD in every cell of my body   Help me to Feel my friends Whole again, and Receiving

within each and every unHealed cell of their body the Light they Already ARE!   Help me to allow

these dear ones to carry out their Contracted Choices in the manner they have chosen and Help

them to Feel that they no longer need to have and to carry such karma as this; that such karma

is over and has been over for many many years now in this realm . . .

The End.   What does this mean, The End?   Since I can remember - and it is long before this

life I am now living as a human in this Unique Arising of GOD, this Divine BodyEmotionMind -

that I have longed for it to BE The End of a being sacrificing its wholeness here, its sense of

whatever it is as an ego separateness, to us, to feed us, to feed my own ego separateness to

feel alive . . .

It is the most unbearable pain for me, to feel this in my emotional field. I do not know why it is

so painful for me.   And I will tell you, my friends, the Only thing that makes it liveable,

bearable, is to Feel You,   Now,   in this moment, in my body as awareness that All Is Already

LightLoveGod.   Light That Wills, in Remembrance and in True Service, The Giving Of Light to

those who consume You.   GOD Help Me To Feel Beyond, To You Beloved   Amen

The InterGalactic Libraries, one interface with . . .

I would guess most of us have had the experience of coming upon a body that has been hit by a

vehicle and is just left there, . . for many years now I have done Prayer with the bodies I

happen to come upon, and many of them I will move from the roadway.   Many are not fully

Transitioned beings yet, not fully done with the Sacred Body which houses the Soul of this

Being.   These latter I bring home to help.

But most are no longer alive on this plane, no longer "here" or aware in terms of their sensory

mechanisms, no longer in their body; and over the years I've had some really remarkable

informations from these bodies.   In general, when I am passing what for sure is a "dead" body,

I take my right hand and I direct the palm towards this body, and I am given/Given the most

amazing Gifts : there will arise, or I will be shown the presence of, gorgeous luminescent,

translucent, iridescent spheres and discs of Light, fanning sprays of a given color in its

multitude of frequencies - above and all around the body. They are close to the body. And the

colors are not of this Earth, in the sense of the heavy matter Earth, or the "old Earth" who is

so profoundly Evolving into the "New Earth"... but more, the colors are brilliantly sparkling,

JoyFilled Colors of the New Earth. There has been a tremendous range of frequency bands of

Colors shown to me over the many years, from these Beings I have come across.

Such colors as Coral Indigo Purple Lime Green Yellow Peach Silver Vibrant Reds, Greens,

Blues, Pinks, Gold, White. . . spectrums of Colors of Spheres and Discs and dancing Sprays all

about the body. It so Reminds me of the Colors I have Witnessed while working in the Sacred

Body Factories on the remarkable torsos of LightFlesh, of the Rainbows riding high above Us,

spanning the Infinity of the Sacred Body Factories.

And, of great interest to me is the uniqueness of each body's Colorful Offerings. . . although

sometimes when there has been a family hit, say a momma Cooner and her babies or a momma

Squirrel and her weenies, there may be shared Colors as though there are, too Families of

Colors. But this is not always true. There may be one offspring who has completely different

array and intensity of frequencies expressed about the body lying there.

I have also experienced this with bodies on mortuary slabs, in anatomy classes, during surgeries

and explorations within the cavities and organs of beings here. I worked for some time as a

Pathology Assistant during which I did numerous autopsies on elderly folk, criminals, babies,

young adolescents, adults ... all had the same Glowing, Evanescent, Iridescent and Luminous

Discs and Spheres about them - which did not change in intensity or presentation during the

autopsy or exploratory/research investigations. However, what did change was that as we were

doing our explorations, new Spheres and Discs might appear from within the cavities of the

beings to float up and out to the surface; and upon suturing closed, might remain there or return to the cavities they arose from.   Never was I afraid of these beautiful energies, these

Gifts. Just totally in Awe. I never told anyone what I was experiencing as it did not feel safe at

the time. However, with the Earth Changes, the Ascension Processes, the never ending

amazing "findings" about our Universe, our Earth in these days, I feel safe to share with you.

Thank you.

Over the years I have asked for Insight with regard to these deeply Sacred Offerings that Arise

and seem to stay there for days and days with the bodies on the roads – and even when the

body is no longer there, the Nodal Template informations remain. There is no fading, no

lessening of the intensity and, as time has passed, more and more carry New Earth expression;

more and more I am given to see gem-like, Crystalline Light, Colors glowing and radiating from

within these Sacred Discs and Spheres.   And more and more recently too I am shown fan-like

sprays of DiamondLight of many hues rising up from the Nodal Cores, up up merging with the

higher Levels of Vibration - again, Creations and Manifestations of the New Earth Soul/Body

Matrices;   these Loving Creations of the Sacred Body Factories we are all Co-Creating LOVE.

And what has come in is this, and I am told it is by no means all that is going on with these

Spheres and Discs and Sprays of Light : the Sacred Vessel inhabited by the Soul aspect of

each Being has related to it certain Colors that correspond to its "Unique Expression" as well

as its "Unique Job" (Destiny?) here on Planet Earth. These Colors are also, after the body has been vacated by the Soul aspect, yet still resides within the Node, collected Information by the Earth and by the InterGalactic Libraries. The Color Full Information of particular frequency bands carry the unique experiences / evolution of the being and are downloaded, and data retrieved, by the Earth Herself and by the InterGalactic Libraries. In this way information concerning what "happened" in this unique life here in this Ego Field can be stored in Earth's Sacred Body and retrieved as necessary in the Creation of a new Unique Sacred Body and Node layered onto the preexisting Template for that Soul; thus there is a bridging between previous Body Nodal experiences and Creation of the New Sacred Body & Node within the Soul's Template of Experience/Love.

And obviously, too, collation and comparison among individuals among groups among species among Kingdoms can be done with analysis using the high Technologies of Light, Love Imbued, to help determine what is going on as regards change/evolution/experiences of the trillions of beings inhabiting the Sacred Bodies and Sacred Nodes. There are, as with coming into the body here, the need for stepwise changes in frequencies... the Color Full Spheres and Discs contents which go into the Earth (even as She Is becoming Enlightened HerSelf) may be a step down fashion of frequency releases, so She can Feel/feel where we "are" and "have been" and can accommodate changes that will be present in our next presentation here as Body & Node. The Color Full contents which go into the InterGalactic Libraries are stored "as is" and transported back to the Sacred Body Factories for data retrieval and use as needed. There may be, in the next round of Sacred Body Sacred Node Template, a "stepping up" of frequencies if this is what the Soul Contracts for and if karma allows; there may also be a "stepping down" of frequencies in the Sacred BodySacred Node Template if this is what is Chosen and Contracted for by the Soul.

Over days the body goes through its processes of returning to Earth, the material, the molecular, the atomic earth with the help of organisms that have evolved here to aid this process called "decomposition"... the returning to the material from which it is made, chemical molecules and atoms, dirt, dust; from which in this Ego Field we tend to turn away and have terror around for we are, by design and choice, so deeply identified with our ego-I and its separative, certain to "end" ways. The Sacred Body "dies" The cellular Lights go out The amazing organization and structure inherent within the Sacred Body as matter, ends. It is all part of the Experiment and the Creation of a Sacred Vessel experiencing separation from What Lives It... at least until we choose - like Earth HerSelf, with the Ascension Process fully underway, enabling the Sacred Body within Its Sacred Node - to Live As Light here, Now.

The Cells, the Molecules, the Atoms, the Dark Matter Made Light All Alive All Changing Infinitely All Loving Self ONE With What Constantly Ceaselessly Creates It

And so I feel and Feel it is about Choices : the Color Filled Spheres, Discs and Sprays of Light Brilliant and so Glowing and Actively Serving! They are Conscious, this I Feel without question!

Even though the body, the traumatized, neglected, over serving body lies there - so much

LOVE is pouring forth from this demise! In every instance I am astounded, there are no words

to express what happens in my unHealed heart / my Healing Heart. Thank You God for this Gift

which helps me to tolerate, accept, ALLOW, for Evolution as it is, as it needs to be, as is being

Chosen by so many here, NOW and in the "past" the ego past which is fading fading . . .

Amen

The "apparent Not so Sacred" Body Factories

What do we mean by Sacred?   And, what then might be not so Sacred?   For myself, the crux of the meaning lies in my relationship to Feeling Love, or to not Feeling Love.   When we are Feeling Love, which I have written about extensively in my book self Love and the Healing of Our Animal Friends,[3] you will notice I start with "self Love" and follow this with what might happen when we Love the self : it is not by any means that it is only our Animal friends who can be profoundly helped in their Healing when we Love the self; we ourselves spontaneously Heal, and anything or anyone we come in contact with - are in Loving Relationship With - will be Feeling the Love and Healing themselves too, if they want to. It is, again, about Free Will, Choices,   and also importantly, Where Is My Attention Focused?

When I say the "apparent Not so Sacred" Body Factories the first word I am using is "apparent" which is a word that is useful to inherently describe anything, anyone, any event field that arises within the Ego field, where we are all exploring in a shut down, cut off from Feeling Love/self Love, contracting away from Love.   Experiences that arise when we are feeling so cut off and egoically isolated result in "apparent" experiences, for they have a lessening of Clarity and Discernment, and are loaded with distortions that are mirrored-back to us in every moment of egoically contracted existence. I have always really liked the phrase in the Bible, "Through A Glass Darkly" as this is to me exactly what is going on; we are not

Seeing with our Heart Clarity, we are seeing with our phenomenologically limited senses.

This is true for all living things here. It is our choice to explore in this way, which is fine if this

is what we want to do! But, in any moment, if we so wish, if we so Choose! we can place our

Attention on the Love Prior to the Glass Darkly, the egoic mirrors we are creating when we do

not Love the self... and lo and behold we begin Again to Remember Feeling Love. This Is A

Given, 100%! And it is available to All, All the Time! In each moment, NOW, and NOW, and if

you forget and slide back down that slippery ego self denying and unLoving slope... NOW,

again and again, NOW...

It is just a matter of Choosing, in Each Moment, to Attend to the Love That Lives Everything

Here, and Has Lived Everything Everywhere Infinitely.

And, so when we say the "apparently Not so Sacred" Body Factories we are speaking very

directly to the egoic, shut down, unFeeling, unLoving way of relating to All that IS Sacred, Here,

Now, in every moment if we would but Attend!

This is true for the medical doctor doing surgeries, for the animal rights activist shouting down

with indignation and hatred another being who has a different, uniquely different, way of

relating to animals; this is true for the child all alone in her bed at night when her parents are

ignoring her and she is beginning to feel so unloved, not heard, not cared for, and especially not

validated by the ego neediness getting fed. This is true for the predator who is stalking the prey (plant/animal/human/other)... in each moment it is the RELATIONSHIP TO THE SACRED

VESSEL YOU ARE IN AND THE APPARENT OTHER IS INHABITING that is critical, critical,

Critical.   No excuses.   Either you Love or you do not Love; yourself the apparent other.

And so, there are, in regard to all this, some very interesting and yes, disturbing evolutions on

this Planet rooted in not paying Attention To The Love That Lives Us : some of the most

obvious are war, famine, extinction, holocausts, murder, suicide, genocide, unfeeling slaughter

of beings as a daily routine, experimentation on the bodies, the emotions, the minds of living

entities, crystalline, plant, animal, human - the list has grown to be almost endless here in our

Created Ego Field based on our unLoving choices. For we did, we have been, we are, Choosing.

How much do we ignore the Earth HerSelf in many of these horrendous endeavors egoically

driven through our fears?   Pray our choices become with greater and greater Consciousness

and Loving Intention. And, no self judgment here! Love, self Love here!

For me, in my own truly still Healing Heart and Mind, all of this unLoving relationship to our life

here is unnecessary as a way of existence. There is, as pointed out, no Love in relationships

based on fear, isolation, judgment of self/apparent other... on and on and on

And, of course, there is that ole Famous Triad energy here : Victim Perpetrator Rescuer

upon which the ego - isolated, constantly needy and needing validation of itself for it cannot

Love itself, depends. That ole ego of mine, that mechanism created for exploring what it is like to NOT Feel The Love One IS!

Another very interesting fact I have been aware of for many years now is that in truth there is no real "extinction" in the sense that the Print for the Sacred Body the Sacred Node is stored via the InterGalactic Libraries within our Universes. In another sense, since everything "changes" and in fact we could say that Love Is Change, that Love Is Consciousness that is Creating Constant Change. . . yes, in this sense in each moment All Becomes Extinct as the Energies are ReBorn ReCreated into the New. It is a paradox around which the mind, that ego mind we have developed beyond anyone's dreaming possible! - simply cannot wrap itself. Like everything the Physicists and Astrophysicists are Creating with their profound Minds and Hearts and Numbers these days! Whoooowiiiieeee!

What a trip this is! A Sacred Trip This Is! So, when we find ourselves judging how poopy this place is, how horrific this place is, how awful we treat each other, the animals, and the other profound beings of Nature... Well, what about it?! What IS MY RELATIONSHIP TO these arising here? Why am I Judging them? Why am I judging myself - for that is what it all is, really. Looking into the darkened mirror that I am CoCreating with my Divinity while Not Feeling my Divinity, my Sacredness. Judge Judge Judge oh, even that is a delusion and not real...

Well, let's take a breath and step back and turn to Feeling again, shall we?   I am here.   I Love

you/You.   I Love me/Me.   I Love.   I Choose To Be Love First, that's all.   Thank You God!

---

[3] selfLove and the Healing of Our Animal Friends, Betsy Adams, Balboa Press, 2012

Heart Bursting Open...

Heart bursting open Brain splits   The Axe   The Gun   Stunning blow   My knees bending

beneath me   Blood of my Blood   Soul of my Soul   My friend, I kneel before you and hold your

turmoil in my hands   Hands of GOD I acknowledge   I Yield   I allow your choice   My hands

bleeding and screaming and recoiling in Primal rage, fear, feeling Your Choice   Resistance to

sharing your agony of bodyemotions is so profoundly deep in my cells that Even Now The Light...

OH LIGHT, OH LIGHT ENTER ME,   Release me from this unHealed bondage to this unHealed

emotional body I have carried for millennia   No longer separate from You dear dying sacrificial

unHealed friend   Over and Over unHealed to give of oneself in such a manner.

OH LIGHT, OH LIGHT ENTER ME,   Compassion my Soul to Surrender, To Yield to What Is

Longing to Live me   Healing within me this unnecessary slaughter   Ending this giving over of

the body heart   Soul to slaughter   Over and Over and Over the billions arrive embryonic

emblazoned with the Star on the brow of stunned and stunned

The absolute, deep and profound shock of this existence here, so deep in shock of this

existence here   No feeling,   No,   No more feeling   No more pain and agony and remembrance

of the shared stunning   Do you want to continue in this manner of waking dreams of this dead,

stunned state, of existence?   Existence?

What Existence?   For GOD did not go anywhere   GOD is forever   HERE, NOW, In This Moment

Divine   Can you not rise up, out of this Stuporous state of forgetting   Move toward the

Radiance that IS   Embodied here, Now,   In this realm of chosen forgetfulness -   It is our

unconsciousness, chosen in order to obliterate the pain, to keep us munching and crunching on

old suffering and deadened patterns   When will we allow the Light to Flood   to Clarify   to

Purify   to BE Who We Really Are?   Dear Friend of my ego's shattered heart, Rise Up and

Allow the Light   the Love   the Truth that pre-exists this realm of deadly recurrent dreaming -

Do Not Forget!

Remember, dear Friend, Remember!   We have been so deep asleep!   Come with me from this

slippery blooded floor of coma   Come with me back to the fields in which we Dance, Any Way..

You know,   just dance, Any Way   Tails swinging   Ears flopping   Butts Bucking   Heads

swiveling   Side to Side   We sidestep Back into the Light - Into the Love which IS Always

Any Way Already Here!

Giving Light To Those Who Consume You . . .

There is about you, dear friends, in every case I behold you, a wonder at your unique body

creation of GOD : A standing about, a placement upon the Earth, a sense of Settled In to

whatever it is that you are here for...

Is there no anger in you? No resentment? No yearning for other ways to share your body,

your emotions, here in this Realm?

It is this being domesticated that has always been for me the hardest to comprehend; that you

so totally give over, have given over for millennia... my own rages about this, my own stomping

and storming about on this Earth in regard to this, this, ... And, of course my own egoic

identification with this...

What? Victim? Prey? Stupid? Stuck? Passivity? In the face of the unLoving use of

your unique bodyemotional field, your unique "personality" based on lifetimes of meandering

through this realm, as do I, partaking of the Ego Field - this field of living in isolation from the

very Source that Created Us?

Which, being "domesticated beings" in your case means potential slaughter, utilization of your

body for energy in the form of "food" - the giving up of your unique presentation, here, to

body parts, which are, in turn consumed by others...

So that apparent "others" in their own unique arisings of energies here, can, ... An energy of

manipulation of matter, perhaps?   Or the moving about of energies that manifest and arise

here, which come and go in different spatial and time relationships?   Which arise as unique

presentations of egoic resonating bodies within this Ego Field of manifestations Created within

the Sacred Body Factories...

What IS the difference between us then?   GIVING LIGHT TO THOSE WHO CONSUME US?

How appropriate is it to allow sharing Light through consuming bodies, conscious/not conscious,

that arise here?   What is the True Intent of a Soul manifestation of a being who through its

own Free Will Choices comes here to have its body utilized so unLovingly by others :   To have

its bodymindemotional field abused, raped, bred, molested, coddled, embraced, beat,

manipulated in never ending experimentation by the unFeeling mind, the unHealed Emotions,

until it drops...   How appropriate IS this Choice?   And more importantly, what is required to

create another manner of existence, in which such display of the lack of self Love is so

apparent?   In which such display is no longer necessary?

How I resonate with the title to the book, "The Faraway Horses"[4]   Yes, who would not like to

be far, far away, out of body, spinning off and out of here,   away away from the ego-created,

totally lacking in selfLove, patterns that have arisen in this Realm?   By, I must keep reminding

myself, our own choices...   And it is True, for me, that in this very moment, I can Choose to

Turn to self Love, turn to the Love that Pre-Exists this battered unHealed Realm, and just plain Surrender Up all that is Not Love...   This too is my free will choice, totally.

As a child I would look upon a piece of meat in wonder that it lay upon my plate.   My favorite was pork loin, especially the most succulent hard to reach pieces next the backbone, there... My brother and I would fight over this, mom being the arbiter...

Before, there was a lot of guilt that arose when I could feel in my body the desire the craving the longing to consume the being that only yesterday was my friend rooting about in our farmer fields, or standing by the fence with huge soft eyes gazing so lovingly at me as I rode by on my two wheeler, down the road from our house in Vassar, Michigan. And then there were the Visitations to the Illuminated Field and Woods and Gully behind my house, there, on the other side of the fence line where all was Never Dying Always Living ONE and Filled, Filled with the Feelings of LOVE of GOD . . .   The Sacred Body Factories Incarnate, Lived By and With my tiny child's body   Sacred Body   Sacred Node   Oh! Gift![5]

And now, Remembering, ReVisiting,   Being. . .

----

[4]The Faraway Horses by Buck Brannaman, the Lyons Press, 2003; also available in Audio CD

[5]please see the Nature section of my book self Love and the Healing of Our Animal Friends

It Is Winter, When the Soul Rests...

It is winter, when the Soul rests in the body, breathes in   breathes out   more deeply the

pure whiteness of the Internal becomes the pure whiteness of the External   The Skin One with

both sides of this experiencing / Unzip this precious, Sacred Cloaking - step out of this

Divine Skin Of Life /   Here : What is here?

What does it mean to be here, to Be, to Be Here?   Inside this Sacred Body made forThee

with Hands & Hearts of exploratory Love?

There are many levels to these Divine Body Factories, many millions,   nay, trillions of them,

All over the Universes   Accommodating the trillions and trillions of Souls Yearning to explore

as "form" as "manifestions" of Bent-Light, the Creative Veering Away by Choice, by Free Will

from the ONE, That Perfection of the Formless Creating Form in Infinite variety for Infinite

explorations of Manifesting Love, GOD, ONE . . .

The human Sacred Body is but one expression of this Yearning to manifest, to incarnate.   The

Earth, HerSelf is a Divine Sacred Body - Her Soul exquisitely in Alignment with Learning to Be

Love, to Be, Here, Now   To Be Love first in each Moment that is Truly the Divine Gift of the

Breath   Which She Shares unstintingly with all the living forms who have come to live upon, and

within her Sacred Manifestation. . .

And, so, again - What is it to be here, Now? To Be, to have created for you, for me, for

each of the Trillions of Souls this Incarnation / as Sacred Form :

An Expression of Divine Love EMBODIED : Who "makes" us?   Who "devises" us? Who is it

that Feels Us Into Manifestation? It is Eons beyond thought   It Arises from the Sacred Heart

of the Cosmos, a gift, A Surrendering of Love Into Love Manifest

The Vessel, You I We   Us   Created precisely   meticulously   accurately in Alignment with

each Soul's Yearning / With each Soul's Free Will to Manifest, to Inhabit Its Unique Arising of

God, Love ONE

Zip

Unzip

Come In

Go Out

And Thus The Beloved Is ALL There Is, the Remembering is a Divine Gift held permanently

within the Breath, and thus within the Heart Forever and Ever -   The Awakening to the fact

that we are Not separate, that we are not only the form in which we "reside," at least for now,

for this particular exquisitely profound Journey we are Choosing in Each Divine Moment.

Perhaps here on Earth.   Perhaps here on Sirius.   Perhaps here on Nebula R161.   Perhaps

here within Andromeda as She Merges with Our Galaxy.   Perhaps here with the Angels.

Perhaps here with the Orions.   Perhaps on Nibiru.   Perhaps within Alcyone Oh Radiant One, or

Perhaps within RA. . .   Perhaps we have chosen Outside our "perceived, apparent" Universe,

beyond the Membrane and all its docking Chambers, Chambers of Light, of Transformation to...

to... here, yes, ...

While inhabiting a Unique Arising, a Unique Sacred Form, a Unique Sacred Body of the Divine

Of All That Loves Us

Zip

Unzip

In

Out

What goes before the Zip   What comes after the Unzip   What is here? Now? Oh Sacred

Body of My Divine Creator, How to learn to Remember,   to Surrender,   To Feel Again What I

Truly AM?   The Unknowable   The Feeling   How wondrous that the ego mind of this Sacred

Vessel Dissolves in the Love, in the Feeling that is Prior to all that is "here," excruciatingly

based in mechanisms that cannot Love itself.

My Prayer : Oh Radiant GOD   In deepest Gratitude for these opportunities to reside within,

be held by   rest within   my forgotten Sacredness Remembering, Whole Bodily Remembering

What is the unconscious, really? . . .

There is profound Joy in experiencing and exploring in a body. There is nothing else like it in all

of Creation.   And, what is of great interest to me is the relationship between the Sacredness

of this Body and the unconsciousness that resides in : the body?   the cells?   the Soul?

??...

Does the Soul remember : Before Zip?   Before UnZip?   After UnZip?

What kind of Technologies of Love, of Love Remembrance provides the Templates for the

Sacred Body and what is "in" ?

What is the unconscious, really?   What happens if Consciousness occurs : in the body?   in

the cells?   in the Soul?

What is this Loving alignment that I Feel, that I personally experience in my whole Body All the

Time with God   &   my "unconscious" ?

Will the dissolution of the unconscious be the end of the Body as we know it?...   What happens

when the Body becomes suffused inundated   Transformed   by/INTO LIGHTLOVE ?. . .

Is it that we needed the unconscious in order to have the experience of separation from the

Love We Are?   Did the unconscious "grow" based on choices we made, feelings we did not

want to "remember," actions we did not want to be Consciously "responsible for?"...   Even the little Bacterium, the Paramecium, the Aurelia   the tiniest Virus -   All are Blessings of

God and the Sacred Body Factories in the sense they are all Created from God, ultimately.. .

Who or What is "in charge" of Creation of the unconscious? Me? For sure some part if not all

is part of my Free Will Creation within and without my Sacred Vessel . . .   And Jung's

Collective Unconscious, created over eons and eons of shared Ego Field harmonic resonances...

The Face At The Bottom Of The World[6] perceived as "living in darkness," away   away   away

from the Light, the Love,   and which, by its very existence/Existence draws To ItSelf the

Light, the Love, Imploding within ItSelf in Divine Surrender to the Love It Is, and has always

Been -   Waiting, Biding Its Time   for that Merging, that Transformation of LOVE INTO LOVE

And then there is that little one-liner I heard one night expressed from deep within my being as

I Felt the Heart Relationship to the Face At The Bottom Of The World :   "the unconscious is

Love hiding from ItSelf"... but not really hiding, for No thing can hide from Love, from its

Truth ultimately Always Was Conscious, but chose to "forget"   to "hide" from ItSelf   Until...

The Journey of LOVE UnFolding Into LOVE never   never   Ends. . .

---

[6]see my book Face At The Bottom Of The World, Betsy Adams, Rhiannon Press, 1983

More on the Sacred Node

I am shown an image of the Body "being dipped into" the Sense of Separation, what for me I refer to as the Ego Field. I have had for many many years this vision of the Soul – or perhaps more accurately an aspect of the Soul - as being "suspended" in the Ego field, a "node" of unique harmonically resonating frequencies of Light and light suspended in the "DarkLight and the dark" of the Ego Field.

The light of physics, of the light spectrum, as we know it via the ego mind, is not the same as the Light, the Light of En-Lightenment, of the FEELING of God Living One, of the Feeling of God Living the Sacred Vessel while suspended in the Ego Field or even before entrance into the Ego Field. . . Absorption and Absorbsion are not the same as the Frequencies of GOD LOVE, GOD LIGHT. . .   the absorption and absorbsion of physical light, as Einstein and the present day physicists use the term, is not the same as LOVE, the multitudinous, Infinite Vibrations that Exist as Feeling.

And, of course, feeling is not the same as Feeling[7]

The node, or more correctly, the Sacred Node spoken of previously can move about, but is tethered above and below by a series of chords of "Light" / "Energy" that keep it always embedded within the Ego Field but also "kept alive / in Alignment With the Creator"...

And, hence, "kept alive and in alignment with/Alignment With" the Sacred Body Factories; with required informational output and input to insure the Soul aspect inhabiting this Vessel carries out its Free Will Contract with regard to its evolution, and if enough Feeling develops within this Soul and its Vessel, its Spiritual Evolution.

OK, some maunderings here :

The Node is there, suspended in the Ego Field; tethered both ends to the Sacred Body Factories   input/outflow   inflow/output   and of course, gathering of, storage of data

The Node exists between actually Incarnating Sacred Bodies, i.e., this Node has a "life of its own" : It is a "casing" of energy for the Sacred Body, the body that slips into the Node and needs this Node in order to sustain the Body's life, exploration, existence, evolution here in the Ego Field.

The Nodes (and there are trillions) preexist the Bodies

The Bodies inhabit the Nodes

The Soul's aspects inhabit the Bodies

These Soul aspects come and go

The Bodies come and go

And, too, ultimately, when the Node's Job, its Divine Programs and Intents are completed, the Node too goes back from Whence It Came via the InterGalactic Libraries (or, and this is just coming in ... the InterUniversal Libraries) for downloading, uploading, data as experiencial frequencies of Light/light and Love/love

The Body Divine (this is where the genetics, the Darwinian evolution, occurs) also has a quite dependent life of its own that goes something like this: The Body slips into the Node, the Body is a template into which the cells, the infant Body grows...   without the Node there would be no viable Body here, for the infant Body to grow, to change:

An Energetic Casing, ... A *?* here: Do we move from Node to Node as Mother, embryo, fetus, infant?   And this is what I am getting from the Families of Light who work within the Sacred Body Factories :   No, the Mother's Node holds the Sacred Embryo, Sacred Fetus and at birth there is a budding off from this cohabited Node, which becomes for a time "merged energetic fields"...   the one living from the other as the Sacred Infant is completely dependent upon the Mother, Caregiver energetic flows to survive.   Ultimately these merged Nodes "separate" and the Child becomes more independent of the Mother's energetic "feedings" and literally becomes its own suspended Sacred Node with its own Soul aspect inhabiting the Sacred Body. And as noted before, which is of great interest, this new Node may or may not have "familial" characteristics of the Mother Node energetically.   It is the Body genetics which seems to have more frequent similarities/samenesses of energy bands harmonically shared.

And perhaps of interest here?   "We all have the same ego"   i.e., we all share, harmonically, Ego Field vibrational frequencies, we all share the unconscious harmonic resonances here... Each one of us as a Soul aspect, is unique vibrational frequency bands suspended within this Ego Field, and whatever we are in harmonic resonance with, we are "aware" of, we"share," - literally harmonically share with the "perceived other" in our CoCreating Ego Field.   This is of course true for the Node as well as the Body, the Nodal frequency bands being, of course, less dense than the Sacred Body frequency bands.

Everything is Provided within this Egoically Resonating Hall of Mirrors for us to experience evolution here, via the Contractual Free Will Choices each of our Soul's aspects have made before incarnation here; before inhabiting our Sacred Bodies and our Sacred Nodes.   It is evident that any given Soul can have many Soul aspects presenting here... and something Michael said that resounds :   "Actually, there are really only 8 Beings on this Planet."[8]

Consider the ramifications of that!!

And finally, the Ego Field per se, being a creation of the Sacred Body Factories, with the constant inflow/outflow of experientially based data each Soul's aspect creates on each journey... nothing is ever "lost" or "wasted" or "ends"..... All, just like the bodies here the deeply material Light filled Bodies here   is recycled and either uploaded or downloaded for the next Incarnation.   Gratitude   Gratitude   Gratitude

Where we are now, with the highly evolved systems of "Nodal Containment," "Templates" and Budding-Offs and Creations of New Nodes...   all of this is way beyond how it all "started" way back eons and eons and trillions and trillions of years ago in our Universe's "timing" . . .

Cycles and Cycles and Eons and Eons. . .

And, this last is way beyond me, my comprehension.   The Sacred Bodies, the Sacred Forms, the adaptation of the Forms to the "feeling of being separate from the Love" and the actual survival, i.e., staying within the Sacred Form and not leaving this Form to return to the Love Remembered - over and over and over!! Agonizing feelings that incur upon our Chosen Sacred Separation.

And so it is not a bad thing to feel separate   It is not a bad thing to forget   It is not a bad thing to be here, in the Ego field -   We NEED TO REMEMBER THIS!!

It is not a bad thing to be on Earth, in a Body, navigating and exploring and evolving as we are. And truly it is not a bad thing to be here in these times of Great Change, of Earth Changes.

It is a GIFT that you, each of you, that I, that we all Be Here NOW and what really matters as far as I am able to feel/Feel is what is our Relationship to what we have Co-Created in our lack of Remembrance... How we Feel about ourselves How it is absolutely critical that we learn to stop judging the self for Not Remembering and for all the unLoving "consequences" that have arisen that we have Created while Asleep. It is just part of a profound Cosmic Experiment in which each Unique Divine Soul CHOSE to explore and experience . . . and it is Time Now in these Times of Great Changes for Us All to Awaken, Remember the Love We Are! That's all. . .

The brain as well as other parts of the Sacred Body have built into It, portions that are always a fast track to the Feeling of the Love We Already Are, before Incarnation, before feeling so alone in our separation from the Beloved. It is built in, and but needs our Attention placed upon these built in Frequencies of Love, built in Frequencies of Home. We are not and never have been, alone. How many Thousands upon Thousands of Helpers we each have! It is beyond my ego mind to comprehend, but it IS FEEL-ABLE. This Love We ARE, Have Been Forever

---

[7]please see my recent book selfLove and the Healing of Our Animal Friends for discussion of love/Love, feeling/Feeling, unique/Unique, breath/Breath etc

[8]Michael Innocence to the author - I would like to mention here that I was shown in the DreamTime & on other Levels the Nature of these 8 Beings. More to be written on . . .

For Some Reason, I Feel Like I'm In Training...

THIS IS A TRUE STORY

One day I drive by this farm where my friends the cows live, and I count 6 young steer and 12 elder steer The next day I drive by this farm where my friends the cows live, and I cound 0 young steer and 16 elder steer The next day I drive by this farm and there are NO steer at all! And then, even only 5 hours later I drive by and there are 12 young steer and 12 elder steer!... Now, look here, this farmer's barn is barely big enough for 12 of each animal as big as 12 elder steer, let alone adding in 12 younger!

But I tell you the truth, the honest truth of my own experience: this has happened over and over to me when I visit this farmer's place and my friends - one day a few, the next day a lot! The next day zero! All over the holograms All over the map!

For some reason I feel like I'm in "training" - whatever this may mean. Like I am being Boinged around so I can't get attached to any one presentation of my friends manifesting as Sacred Bodies here. I am not "allowed," or I am perhaps not "allowing myself" to settle into one thing or another as things arise and end on this plane, on this Planet Mother Earth. I am learning how to truly Relate to the Comings and the Goings, the beginnings and the endings, the constantly changing arisings of GOD here as manifested in these particular, these Unique bodymindemotional dear dear friends the cows... (And, in some ways it seems that for all they are doing to help me here, perhaps capital "Cows" capital "Steer" would be more

appropriate?)

I am being Given, I Feel, a wondrous opportunity to feel in my human emotional field what it is

like to "lose" my friends before I "lose" them to slaughter and to discover my new friends

All the time! Now Now and NOW!... They never really "go" anywhere! More, it feels like

they are coming and going across the dimensions or borderlands or passing through some great

divide within the holograms, ...or something! Who knows?! I really do not understand at all!

I just sit here by the fence and count the cows/Cows. My eyes are bugging out My heart is

all aching and terrified and feeling all alone again on the days of zero friends and then it

bursts open with joy and we dance together in our God given and Replenished bodys when there

are, for some reason, All of Them Back!

Whatever this means

So, I admit it is out of my hands It is out of my control They come and they go And

sometimes I can feel their bodies inside of me, after,... Especially after the ends of their

Sacred Bodies as an integral unit. Their bodyparts float and shift about within me, filled with

LIGHT filled with LOVE Filled with the LOVE these beings have for the ones they are feeding.

And the bodyparts as they flow through the one who Receives, feel/Feel as though they are

Blessed

Truly

And so, it feels as though my part in all of this is just that I try and Feel my way as to what is, in this Moment of Feeling, the Truth of a True Loving Gesture : What IS the appropriate Love Filled Gesture I can give my friends on the other side of this fence? What can I do to help them Feel the Love They Already Are, and to carry that Love to slaughter,... if they must, if they continue to so choose,...

Do they remember? Will they remember? Do They Remember? Will They Remember?

Do my dear friends the cows/Cows steer/Steer LOVE themselves, the True Self that preexists this temporary arising of the One that they present : there on the other side of the fence, bobbing their wondrous heads, the deep brown eyes Soft and Receiving and Giving and again Receiving the Light The Love The Feelings of Being One That We Are?...

Yes

And Yes

And YES

As they say, Theory is one thing...

THIS IS A TRUE STORY

As they say, theory is one thing, experience and feeling the experience is another thing

altogether...

About 4 days ago there were zero cows in my neighbor farmer's field and zero in the barn.

Overnight from 24 to zero!   Just like that!   Well, in spite of all the "lessons" I just wrote

about and shared with you,... in spite of all the Metaphysical hoopla created in my ego mind, to

help me feel I might "understand" -   I lost it, as they say.   I cried and I cried and then called

my friend, a human friend, to share

And at the end of this sharing, we both said at the same time, I bet when I go back there they

will all be back!   And five hours later, returning from visiting clients, they were all back!   Now,

how is this possible!?

One thing I need to make clear, is that the field where the cows go is totally visible from the

road, and there is a railroad track at its farthest end, just outside the fenceline ... so when I

saw zero, it was, on this plane, "really" zero. And I can see entirely inside the barn from the

road, and there were zero cows in there earlier too...

85

The resistance I have to accepting that this is happening to me all the time now; I call them

hologram shifts for lack of a better way to describe the comings and goings and the feelings

and the wonder and awe of it all. But no matter what, I Feel it is a Gift.

Well, today, this morning, when I realized that all but 6 of the steer had "really" gone to

slaughter and were in fact no longer on this plane as integrated and whole Sacred Bodies, I

broke down again.

Something had changed -   there would be for this Moment, no Boinging around... i.e., it had

become very very necessary for me to pay attention, to Attend, as Lovingly and as Gently as I

could to how it really feels to me, to my ego, to my emotional beingness here, when I feel all my

friends dead in the sense their Soul is no longer inhabiting the beloved body, to which my own

bodyemotions is so attached.   When I just feel the end of the beloved arising of my friends...

For some reason, this time I broke down into the deepest despair and depression I have had in

a very very long time   And I cried out to God, to Michael to please help me   Help Me!   I

breathed in   I breathed out   And I imagined the Light and Love pouring into me, into every cell

of my being as I breathed as deeply as I could.   Which was not very deep at first because of

my whole body being clenched against feeling the pain!

Clenched and held and tight and NOT Wanting to Give Way before the pain   Held and Tight

And the Breath,...   Remembering that in spite of all this holding on... all this resistance to

Receiving the LOVE...   Remembering   Remembering that Love Comes First, before everything

Resisting   Breathing   Resisting   Breathing

And in spite of all my tight control against feeling this pain, of my ego's battle against Feeling

The Love The Light   GOD...   I turned with deepening Consciousness to the Communion, . . .

Choosing to Breathe   Choosing to become as relaxed and Receiving of the Breath as I could...

Choosing to Receive GOD LOVE as best I am able In This Moment . . .

I Breathed...   And within 20 seconds All Pain Was Gone!

Just Like That!

What?   What?   Where did the pain go?   How is it possible that there be such a flushing away

of such a deep agony from my emotional field in so short a time?   It astounded me!   It still

astounds me!   I sat up from my hunched over place, my hands tight against my heart, terrified

I would begin feeling that pain again...   And Breathed again,   no pain...

I want to try to describe this clearly here, because to me it is a True Miracle in my life here -

for it has been hard for me to feel, or perhaps it is better to say, it has been hard for me to

ALLOW myself to feel because of all the pain I have experienced in this lifetime, in this realm

(and who knows how many other lifetimes in how many realms along with this one?...)

My cells, my body, were still laden with the weight of the depression I have not felt

Consciously for so long... years years ago...   But, in this moment, this Miracle, my body was

still feeling heavy but all around me the emotions of a very light sort were peacefully

permeating me, tender tender And I could feel in my cells the memory of this Joy, this

Peace.   My cells, in spite of this heavy bodily feeling, Remembered!   It was, and still is, a

Miracle.

And so I Breathed again   and again   more deeply and more fully the Light and the Love into my

dear body   into the cells   into the intercellular matrices   so filled with memories of so many

lifetimes of ...   of...   Every human, every animal   every living thing here knows whereof I

speak...

And after about 5 minutes even my cells were at peace, my whole body relaxed, suffused.   My

body felt "empty" of the depression and the despair and hopelessness which had permeated my

life until now

Loving in this Realm of :

All the comings and the goings   All my ego attachments to the comings and the goings   My

attachments to my self as it arises here   My self's (ego's) investments in keeping alive its

senses of separation, of this sense of "self," with its related deep investments in its created

sufferings, and the little love that in turn comes and goes   It IS Coming   It IS Going   I am   I am Not   I am I am NOT   I AM NOT separate, Always, The Breath IS The Light LOVE GOD

IS

And IS

And so the Song :   God Bless the animals and all that arises here,   wonderously arising as

unique forms, Unique Manifestations of GOD...   Where is my attention / My Attention

focused?   I AM That Upon Which My Attention Is Focused

I AM That Which PreExists This Realm,   While still, wondrously arising arising over and over

within this Sacred Realm . . .

GOD BLESS US ALL   GOD BLESS GOD   DO NOT FORGET!!!

Today I awoke with a bit of anger around...

THIS IS A TRUE STORY

Today dear friends I awoke with a bit of anger around, If it is so fucking easy to release all this pain then why did I have to go through it all in the first place!? I was, my ego was, really mad! let me tell you... and of course I wanted "to know" why in the hell all my friends the animals, and their friends the humans, have to go through so much pain...?? To what end?

Well, guess what! I do not know. I don't know. I can conjecture that perhaps it has to do with the "evolution" of this Planet and all the species on it... and so on and so on... that our pain is our goad, as my dear friend Michael has pointed out... and I do not feel I can blame my friend for so Lovingly pointing out Truth as He Lives It.

So, let's say that pain is a way of speeding up our evolution here, that without pain we just sit about being Blissed and going nowhere Or better yet, let's try and see what it feels like to just say I don't know and let it go at that?

And so dear friends, I laid back down and I allowed myself once again to feel the anger, the rage, the betrayal, the sense of being "slipped a Mickey" I allowed myself to feel how stupid I felt at my own culpability, of being so easily led about by my senses of victimization, feeling abused by others (and of course by my own self), allowing myself to be abused.

I allowed myself to fall into the feeling that it is OK ...   I allowed myself to just embrace that I just do not know   That it is OK to not know and just feel whatever it is that I am feeling

No Matter What

And I chose to breathe in the Light again   the Love   GOD I chose   And as before, within seconds my emotions were clarified!   Yes, It works!   Just like that it works!

So, it comes down to this for me :   I guess it is up to me to choose what I will do from here on...   For, it is true that the more my emotional field clears, and my body clears, there is a deeper and deeper sense and Feeling that I am truly separate from nothing : That everything here can be Felt As One, even though to my brain, and my bodymind senses, all "appears" as separate arisings, "outside" my self sense.

So, I feel I will just accept this realm, and do my best to learn to Truly Love myself.   That one of my lessons here is to learn to Allow my self to feel how my emotions feel, and to Feel what is Always Here, Now in this Divine Moment : Love.   And I realize it takes time for all this. Even though every time "IT" happens to me, IT is a total Remembrance of my "Natural State;" My Natural State Of Being Love.

It takes time for the body, for the emotions, and for the mind in its Earth bound frequencies, to become clarified and to deeply, profoundly, be able to Feel in every moment Whole Bodily.   It happens in stages, and is a Unique Awakening for each of us... no two beings here in this

realm are exactly the same, each a Unique Arising,   each in the One Heart . . .

So, I Surrender.   I Allow   I Yield   I Give Over   I Choose to Become One With What Lives Me,

I Choose the Divine Union of this Moment

And Thus ends

All this agony of feeling separate   From you   From Me   Of needing to attach to you in some

way so I don't feel so all alone, here in this body;   Oh Dearest GOD   Help me to Feel, To Be!

Passivity / The Yin Space

How it feels as though the cows with the depth of their domestication, are modeling a potential

for the Healing of passivity, for the presentation here of the Healed Yin Space. How, by their

just being the energy they are - seeming to hold a space of stillness, groundedness, slowness

Potentially mirroring, and with Love Infused, the Yielding of the Soul to the Beloved; while

simultaneously mirroring the fear, the contraction away from Love, this sense of being separate

and alone within a body separate and alone from all other bodies...melded into the herd. . .

And so vulnerable   a body so very Vulnerable

Passivity resides within contraction, an unconscious withholding away from Source, which

Births us endlessly   unconscious   un-Receiving   feeling unLoved   unwanted   agonal

Searching   :   The Yin Space   /   Passivity

These energies are nothing alike, except within the confused ego self, separated, foundering,

cut off and lost among created herd survival mechanisms. . . crowding together for safety and

a sense of "what to do next" . . . no individuation, and yet... Each Is A unique arising here,

This Is A Given : Remembering

To breed an animal for these characteristics, and to cull from the herd those who "talk back,"

who "won't take it," who express potential individuation -   learning in the depths of this culling, genetically the consequences of "standing out," of "demanding space," of being

reactive to oppression of the self... how we have created passivity so we can control... And

the allowing by the being of this control : choosing to go with the induced passive state for

sheer terror of the consequences of not being "passive" : the "culling from the herd;" the

literal killing of the body, the Sacred Vessel, its removal from the relational sense of self. . .

Generation upon Generation   Lifetime after Lifetime of culling...   no, passivity has nothing to

do with the Yin Space except as a Potential Mirror.

Control, that sense of having control over the power of another, a "perceived other," so we may

do with it what we please, or what "necessity" demands - consumption of this passively

imbued body genetically carved out for our own needs, our own purposes.   No Love, just blank

thoughtless   unconscious need of one body to live parasitically on another.

This parasitism does not consist in just the consumption of another's physical body here in this

realm; this parasitism exists on every level of existence here - mental, emotional, physical

among all the species who have chosen to explore how it feels to Not Feel.

It is as though we breed vulnerability so we will not be so afraid, we breed within ourselves and

within the perceived others we need to energetically utilize, this passivity so we will not be so

afraid, so that we can control the beast that resides deeply within - the fire, the Yang

Energies that simmer beneath, deeply within all passivity . . .

The Yin Space holds within It The Source, Soft Yielding Surrendered, and yet Dynamically

Alive, never "passive" For It Breathes Creation Of Itself In Endless Blissful Being Love -

Revealed Within And Without : The Grace Rapturously Ecstatically Ceaselessly

Constant Re-Union With ItSelf

Passivity   there, do you feel the "clunk" the lowering of energies, submerging, pressing

downward upon the Soul's Expression?   The fading into some night of background deep deep

into dark, unreactivity,   Not allowing the feelings, let alone the Feelings of deserving

expression Here   NOW?

And thus we could say that passivity, the essential energies residing within the domesticated

breeds, is the creation of a mirror   :   That our own Soul learn to feel what it might be like to

be so vulnerable without voice, without deserving to speak or be or exist here within our own

precious expression.   We hold up the breeding mirror before us, and we can choose, now and

now and Now and NOW   to bring the Love into this darkness of inexpressible aloneness or

perhaps to wait another day, another life, another slaughter, another parasitic modality and

mortality,... and another...

No, it is time to return Home   to the Great Mother   to the Great Energy of the Greatest Loving

Feminine Which Always Receives and Gives Lovingly :   The Yin

And when we come back, if indeed we decide to clothe ourselves once again in the Divine

Rainment of the Sacred Body, we can come back with voice, with self Loving Gestures, with a

Consciousness of the Free will that is always available residing in our One Heart.

And so, today, when Meditating   when Sharing   with my dear friends the cows/Cows   with my

dear friends the steer/Steer   with my dear friends you/You   JOY & RADIANCE as we/We

come Bounding and Waggling and Jumping and Twirling within the LightGOD which Creates,

has Possessed   US/THEM,   Our Sacred Bodies Merged Totally Within NeverEnding Feeling of

OurSelves ONE

OH ECSTACY DIVINE

The Forty Horses

THIS IS A TRUE STORY

One day, years ago, I was asked by a lady who lives a long way to the Western Part of the

State, to please come and help her with some 4 or 5 horses of a herd of 40 horses - these 4

or 5 having various chronic behavioral &/or physical conditions she felt needed attending to.

All her horses were auction horses who were heading for slaughter in Canada; they had had

rough, certainly unLoving backgrounds and experiences.   She brought as many home with her

as she was financially able and could all live comfortably in the space she had available.

I made this long trip to her farm happily, for I really like long road trips in my Jeep, and arrived

in the late afternoon at the end of the farm's long winding drive - uphill and big old trees

shading the drive, the breeze among them cooling the very hot day.

As the Jeep slowly climbed the hill, the fenceline of roughhewn old darkened grey wood ran

along on my right. And there, just down the bit of a steep slope in the huge yard were the 40

horses. I stopped my jeep, I opened the windows and all came gently loping to the fence.

And gazed

Everything stopped

Everything

I gently opened my door, got out and slowly walked to the fence, bending down and crossed

through the wooden fence to be with them.   All received me with such gentleness - and all, as

I moved very slowly slowly   slowly   into their Space

feeling them   Feeling Them   among them   Among Them -

Deeper and deeper into the herd they began the dancing in slow eddinging circles about me,

trotting and softly neighing   One by One coming, approaching,   some nuzzling, some brushing

my body with theirs   gently   Gently

Each the preciousness of their Being ONE   ONE the Forty   Each . . .

And I too gently Gently turning circle Gently touching gently kissing -   no holding, just

continuous ecstatic movement tender Loving Circles of Light within Light   Heart Within Heart

One   The forty Horses myself   mySelf The Forty Horses Forever this movement huge

muscular soft Receiving Giving Bodies my Body

Gently   Gently   All became still   None moving away   Just still   The Forty Horses myself

The depth of the Silence   The depth of the Love for me of these beings - This Being

I am unable to Express

To this day   this Dance   My Heart   Never Ending

* * * * * *

When I arrived at the lady's house I told her of the horses and The Dance -   She was not

surprised, saying,   "Yes, my horses are very friendly."   Nor was she surprised that I, never

having been to her home before, just went through the fenceline into the herd, ... what I will

say, into the Light, the Illuminated Heart

The White Wolf : Befriending The Predator

How to befriend the predator, the astounding white wolf within   Who stands at the wood's

edge and howls twice, then moves away   Hidden once again within the deepening treed

pathways of the Soul

*   *   *   *   *

THIS IS A TRUE DREAM

I am walking down the path of the village with my kitty Jewell by my side.   For years now I have

seen the wolf, standing there at the northern edge of our village, at the very edge of the deep

forest.   She only howls twice, no more, then turns and moves back into shadow and the hidden.

Today, Jewell and I both see this wondrous white being, down the long hill where the deepest

woods start.   I say to my friend, See Jewell, there is the white wolf again.   And the white

wolf howls twice, as usual.   But this time Jewell growls.   Beside me, she stiffens, her back

beginning to arch.   I am surprised and say, It is OK Jewell, it is just the white wolf . . .

This time,   this time :

The white wolf turns to face us, no longer displaying only her profile, as though she is aware of

us for the first time in all the millennia we have shared these spaces together...   And by now,

Jewell seems frozen in utter stillness, her back still arched, as onward towards us bounds the white wolf. I close my eyes, for I do not want to see the tearing, rendered bloodied mess I am

about to become, and I do not want to feel this ending to my bodymind.

My eyes sealed shut I can feel the white wolf leap right over me and take Jewell out. Just that.

Take Jewell Out.

There is nothing else, and I can feel just this "nothing" all around me : No wolf   No Jewell

No life   And it is as though my breath has stopped forever.   I am all alone with my eyes

literally sealed shut, as with glue.   I prise them with my fingers   I turn in circles   I reach up

with my hands and try to see with my hands what is happening.   Although in truth I do not want

to see.   Oh No   Not at all   I do not want to see what the white wolf has done to my dear

friend gray kitty Jewell, companion for multitudes of lifetimes and journeys in this realm

Earth.

My eyes simply will not open.   And I keep turning in circles . . .   I seem to remember there

was snow everywhere and winter on our walk   I become angry and desperate and I severely

press my eyelids open,   and finally they do open   And everywhere there is just white snow

No blood   No body   No Jewell   No wolf   So it is true, she was as I felt but could not see,

Just Taken Out.

My whole body is shaking in grief and terror and longing for my old and dear friend -   To have

her returned to me whole and healed and beside me   I am sobbing like a baby   I am angry with

the white wolf who has taken her instead of me   I have to stay here and suffer this loss   I

would rather be dead, not able to feel what I am feeling now.

And then, in the snow ahead of me, a large wooden building appears, dark burnished woods

with beautiful peaked eaves and doors of solid trees gifts to us, here in this third realm of

living   I move towards this building,   and it is as though any will I might have had before is

utterly gone   I just need to move my body as it needs to move, a calling, a moving over this

white casing of life towards the wooden building which is now filling with people from the village

where I live.

I can hear their voices and see and feel the puffs of snow from their breaths as they share

We are all moving towards this meeting that is to take place in the guild hall, in the center, in

the town hall, in this Sacred Center which has appeared in our village.   As I walk I can hear

several of the people discussing how already white wolf has Taken Out 2 humans and 2 animals

from our small village   I hear and feel how hard this is to bear in the hearts of those who are

sharing -   And again, I am astounded.   I had no idea that white wolf had ever even moved from

the edge of her forestwoodstrees. . .I had always felt, until today, this moment, that she was a kind of emblem, almost a statue of great sacredness to our village.   That only on Other Levels

did she intercede for us, interact with us   Never in this world of the bodymind.

And as I listen to the murmuring voices, none is raised in either anger or fear, but only in

compassion and empathy. I realize that even here she is sacred to us, now, in this third realm

of the dear and Great Manifested Mother, Earth.   As I move closer, I discover I am truly not

wrong in feeling this.   My human companions in this village are asking one another how we can

help ourselves and White Wolf to live together?

To Share our space in Loving Relationship...Yes, these are the words and the feelings

expressed...   there is no running for guns, for the bow and arrows.   No calling the animal

control person or the police (and actually the chief of police is one who has lost his son to

White Wolf, I just realize this in this moment of awe and slow gentle awakening. . .)

It is as though, in this moment, the sense is 100% that if we just ask for it from a Loving

Space, All Help Will Be Given.   There is no feeling of doubt in this Heart Of Our Village.   And

in this held Space of the Communion we enter the building, mounting the beautiful stairs of

brown, lovingly offered wood, and fall silent.

Inside these beautifully decorated walls of burnished lights, within this wonderfully warm

sanctuary of wood gifted our village, we are all moving about, gently, praying,   asking with

deepest Gratitude to the One Who Lives Us All, to the Cosmos, to GOD, for the help our Souls and our bodies need to Healing the White Beast who lives among us, who, it seems, elusively

preys upon our bodies and who has now Taken Out 5

And then, in Union and in one movement, the villagers, myself, all move together, climbing the

stairs slowly and in silent prayer to the next level, and stand together gazing, in deepening

awareness and in greater Consciousness of the Love That Lives Us All, towards the North,

exactly where always before White Wolf had lived.   Her deep woods are still there, although

now She is nowhere in sight.   The fields and the trees are silent and still and are filling with

Light. . . Even as this room we are in is filling ever more profoundly with the Light.

Our building we are in is in the West.   And here we are, not huddled   not fear filled,   but in

deep Prayer and Gratitude and Surrender to this Gift of Life.   The Feeling in the beings here,

in this Sacred Space is that All Will Be Well, All IS Well.

On this second floor the walls are themselves tall bright windows, allowing us huge vista now of

the snow filled fields, woods, and the village below

There is a very very deep Roar,   a Deeper Roar and suddenly from the South a great river

comes, crashing Crashing and swirling and cascading along below us, the Waters like

Crystalline Light,   the most crystal clear I have ever seen or Felt before in the third realm.

The Light dances within the Waters, and the Animals, hundreds and hundreds of Animals appear from the East to cross the Waters of the Crystalline River, bounding towards us from East to Our West.

And these Animals are like none I have ever seen before, The cows are cows/not cows with great deep brown leathers and faces of fire and light. Their faces appear to have no physical eyes at all, but we can Feel how clearly they are Seeing.   The horses, which carry one rider who is as big as a house, are each as big as two or three houses! They are deep full brown, glistening Light WithIn, their chest HeartOne, and ridden full-bonded with the human who has melded into Receiving Spaces of bodies encasing Light.   He is not human/is human...   a new kind of Human who has no separation from the Being he is becoming/has Become Sharing the ride, This Coming of the Great Pounding Light And there circling and screeeeing high above us, and swooping down in Greeting is White Owl and on His great back, which is 15 feet long at least, rides in Melding Pleasure and Remembrance the Silver Haired Son of the Police Chief - the song he sings bellowing forth from the huge Heart of him, his body glowing with the Light WithIn his ever Opening Sacred Vessel...   How does one contain/Contain so much Light? How does one contain/Contain so much Love? . . .

With   with . . .

All the domesticated beasts are no longer domesticated, but have the fire and Will of their Own Crossing Over.   There is no fear but only Service, and there, within the herds of no longer beasts of terror and passivity, and longing to be free, runs White Wolf - Across the Great

Crystalline Waters towards us.   She is / is not White Wolf, her body massively molding

joyously to the movement of the dancing of the Crystalline Waters...   and beside her runs the

Gray Jewell, Bounding in Ecstatic Joy . . . Lightbody Opening   Opening . . .

It is not that each body is perceived as separate, but that the Light that moves within and

without the Creation of each Body in each moment dances with ItSelf. . . like the Waters of the

River moving and dancing and in each moment ebbing and flowing in the Creation of ItSelf. . .

And within this swirling mass of thousands of Sacred Bodies the predators and the prey of the

old way now Move As One, fording the River of Crystal Light, leaping in Ecstatic Freedom from

bondage of a once agreed upon sense of being separate from the BeLoved, from GOD.   No

longer necessary the consuming of another's body and emotions and mind in order that there be

balance within the spiraling back and forth upon itself that is the Life current within a Universe

of Duality - An ending to the choice of exploration within this Universe as an arising which has

"forgotten" its Source...   Which has evolved this forgetting and evolves in created fears that

forgetting begets.

All this is ended.   All this is no longer necessary. . .

We all, without a thought among us, with Hearts bursting open in Joy and Love and in Receiving

this Gift of Grace, rush to the doors of our building   Our Breathing and Breathed Building, and fling open the doors, rushing down, down the long steps which are changing from deep brown

wood to crystal, from opaque and masked to Clear, Brilliant Crystalline Rainbows of Colors, as

we race down to share in this flowing mass of thousands of new Birthing animals, new Birthing

humans, new Birthing species

Who have Learned to Love themselves   to Love the self   to Feel again their BirthRight. . .

What Creations await us?   What Creations will we Choose?   What new LifeSources will be

explored as the Light We Are   the PredatorPreyOne   That Light Which . . . oh, ancient heart

oh, unHealed Heart. . .   Listen and Feel this word. . . Consumes. . .

That Light Which Consumes Us All   Which IS Us   OneCreation   morphing Infinitely into

Unique Arisings. . .   and yet,   and yet, . .

And into my Heart Opening to the Love That Is   this comes to me   Consumed / Surrender

to be consumed / surrender   to Be Consumed / Surrender . . . there feels like such a

difference in these two words. . . the sheer terror that resides within the feeling of the ending

of the ego-I, incapable of Surrender.   But Love ItSelf Can Only Surrender, for it has indeed no

sense of separateness from That Into Which It Surrenders.   Oh GOD may that Moment Be,

Now, ForEver Always   Amen

*   *   *   *   *

And, as I awaken from this True Dream, I hear my BeLoved Michael shouting   so Clearly,   with

Great Purity   :   "Remember The Sacred Body Factories!"

This Really Happened!

Afterword to The Sacred Body Factories

And what do you enVision, what do you See   racing and tumbling and billowing and flying and

thrumming thrumming towards you from across this Great Crystalline River?   What Divine Gifts

are coming your way from The Sacred Body Factories which lie within the Very Heart of You?

Will there be the Sacred White Buffalo Calf measuring his short life in such brutality, Rising

now before you, before Us All filled with the Light and the Love He Truly Is, and Was even

during his Sacrificial Contract here on this plane?   Will there be the thundering of Zebra and

Elk and Caribou and Rams with Sheep, and the Coyote Pack howling and screaming in the wind

of their Light Filing Lungs, Hearts, Brains   Re Birthing before You, before Me, Before All Who

dare and Yearn Yearn Yearn to bear Witness to Birthing of Co-Creation that is ongoing, now,

and Now, and NOW within the Sacred Body Factories...

Where we All reside, have always resided, side by side by side   The strangest of creatures,

the Off Planet creatures, the beyond our Universe creatures and life forms, the neighbor down

the road a piece, the kitty gazing out the living room window (the Living Room... Window...),

the horse galavanting back from the field to the barn, the dog racing in circles chasing the tail

of blazening LIGHT LIGHT LIGHT

For ALL are from these Sacred Creative Spaces of Our Hearts, ever ReNewing ever Creative

and Yearning to Explore Love within the Divine Form Co-Created with Our BeLoved :   GOD

Remember   Remember   Shout down the Long Tube that stretches from that hidden Face At

The Bottom Of The World, to Up Up UP   There and There and There   INFINITY   and

INFINITE Are The Sacred Creations of Our BeLoved   Formed   Forming   ForEver Sacred,

Divine Bodies Birthed of LightLOVE